LOST

BUTTE

MONTANA

LOST
BUTTE
MONTANA

RICHARD I. GIBSON

THE
History
PRESS

Published by The History Press
Charleston, SC 29403
www.historypress.net

Copyright © 2012 by Richard I. Gibson
All rights reserved

First published 2012

Manufactured in the United States

ISBN 78-1-5402-0695-4

Library of Congress Cataloging-in-Publication Data

Gibson, Richard I.
Lost Butte, Montana / Richard I. Gibson.
p. cm.
Includes bibliographical references and index.
ISBN 78-1-5402-0695-4
1. Butte (Mont.)--Buildings, structures, etc. 2. Historic buildings--Montana--Butte. 3. Architecture--Montana--Butte--History. 4. Butte (Mont.)--History. I. Title.
F739.B8G53 2012
978.6'68--dc23
2012024389

CONTENTS

PREFACE

B utte's streets try to square the city with its geography and its history, but they fail. Quartz Street takes a jog near my house, to better follow an old mining claim; Broadway runs into the Pit; even Park Street has its kink at Washington. Butte's story, as reflected in the buildings that line and once lined its streetscapes, is jogs and kinks and stops and starts, a crazy quilt in ten dimensions of space and time and ethnicity and attitude and emotion.

Butte gets under your skin. I'm a geologist, and I've been a geologist since grade school—passionate about geology to the extent that I never believed anything else could capture my imagination so totally. But Butte, its people, its buildings and its history did it.

Now I spend my time leading walking history tours and driving the chamber of commerce tourist trolley, working with Butte Citizens for Preservation and Revitalization (Butte CPR), the Mai Wah Museum, World Museum of Mining and whatever else comes along. It gives me a diversity that I never had before and an excitement about Butte's internationally significant history that makes me want to share it. That's the basis for this book.

Some of the history here will be familiar to Butte folks who experienced it directly or who learned it well, but a book called *Lost Butte* cannot be complete without touching on familiar stories: the Columbia Gardens, the expansion of the Berkeley Pit and other older but well-known tales such as that of Frank Little. Some stories here are not so well known, but I hope they entertain and inform. So many books tell Butte's stories that it is challenging to find a new niche; I've tried to do that by focusing mostly on the buildings, their losses, the demolitions and history's circumstances that led to the losses—the stories to which lost buildings connect us. The book is for Butte people, but even more, it celebrates them and their past; as such, it is also for visitors by the thousands who come to marvel at Butte's surviving historic architecture, the physical ties to so much history.

To some extent, the book follows a chronological arrangement, from Butte's earliest years to the present, but this is not a rigorous plan. You'll find the Owsley Block story in the first part even though it was lost in 1973.

As I research Butte history for walking tours and for this book, my mantra has become "there's too much to learn," and this account only touches the surface. The bibliography lists the most important books on Butte, including classical historical works and more recent photographic documentaries. Explore them all.

The support, guidance and friendship of everyone at the Butte–Silver Bow Public Archives made the book possible. Ellen Crain, Lee Whitney, Irene Scheidecker, Mitzi Rossillon, Aubrey Kersting and Kim Kohn all were exceptionally generous with their knowledge and time. I thank them as well for their generous permission to use photographs from the archives' collections. Likewise, Dolores Cooney, Tina Davis and Jim Killoy at the World Museum of Mining were extremely helpful and also gave permission to use photos. I've used a few public domain images digitized by the staff at Butte Public Library; their work is a great benefit to all Butte historians. The Mai Wah Society provided some photos as well.

My tour guide colleagues at Old Butte Historical Adventures, especially Denny Dutton, Bob McMurray and Pat Mohan, shared information and fostered my engagement with Butte history. Bob McMurray allowed photographs in his personal collection to be reproduced here, and thanks also go to Kathy Koskimaki Carlson for her contribution and to Nicole von Gaza for help with the Mollie Walsh story. I also thank Mark Reavis, former Butte historic preservation officer, and Mitzi Rossillon, Julie Crowley, Irene Scheidecker and Mary McCormick for information about Butte's more recent preservation history. Mary McCormick and Mitzi Rossillon provided helpful reviews of several sections. Quotes from the *Montana Standard* and from Stacie Barry are used with permission. Many, many other people, in Butte and beyond, were supportive and encouraging. I appreciate all this help very much. Aubrie Koenig, commissioning editor with The History Press, was helpful and understanding throughout the process of making the book a reality, and Ryan Finn, project editor at THP, polished the text and improved it.

I have no doubt that in trying to unravel part of the skein of Butte's past I've made mistakes (few, I hope) and characterized and interpreted some events in ways that may not match others' views. I've tried to be objective, and if I have missed that mark, I apologize. You can chalk it up to caring about the story-telling buildings that make Butte unique—and for that I have no apology.

INTRODUCTION

This Butte is capriciously decorated with sweet brilliant metallic orgies of color at any time, all times, as if by whims of pagan gods lightly drunk and lightly mad.

—Mary MacLane in
I, Mary MacLane: A Diary of Human Days *(1917)*

Although Butte was the first city in Montana to have a Historical Preservation Commission, you might not know it to look at the town. Much of Butte's past was swallowed up—by the Berkeley Pit, by arson fires in hard times and by well-meaning individuals "improving" in the name of progress.

Boom and bust has *always* been the name of the game in America's largest urban mining camp. Its natives rarely spared time to consider Butte's place in history. Uncounted books have told the stories: Manus Duggan and the 1917 mine disaster, Frank Little's lynching, the Butte Irish and more. But at the time, and for most of the twentieth century, Butte's people had little energy for or interest in saving historic relics. They just wanted to get on with life, and something better was the usual goal.

Progress. Butte was certainly not alone in its attitude that modern is better. In many minds throughout the United States, the very definition of progress meant "out with the old, in with the new." Historic preservation as a concept is largely a late twentieth-century idea, and if it came late to Butte, nonetheless it came.

This is not to say that preservation was nonexistent. One of Butte's earliest restoration projects began after a 1918 Ash Wednesday fire ravaged the 1881 St. John's Episcopal Church. It probably helped that copper king W.A. Clark and his family were partial to that church, even long after they had moved to New York and Los Angeles. W.A. Clark Jr., founder (in 1919) of the Los Angeles Philharmonic Orchestra, funded restoration of one of St. John's important stained-glass windows—the one originally commissioned by his father and executed by Pompeo Bertini, stained-glass designer at the Cathedral of Milan, Italy. Likewise, Butte's Exchange Club members came together in the early 1960s to save and interpret mining memorabilia, from lunchboxes to entire buildings, by creating the World Museum of Mining. But Butte's heritage stood largely vacant, ignored and neglected, or when attention did come, it covered up or demolished and replaced. This situation existed until the late 1980s.

Butte often crosses the fine line between neglect that destroys and neglect that saves. Harsh winters prevented "discovery" by architectural illuminati, at least those who might actually *do* something with a diamond in the rough. Butte's reputation as a dirty mining town, the biggest Superfund site in the nation, likely kept some away as well. Ironically, this lack of attention may have helped preserve the clearest expressions of Butte's raucous past: an underground speakeasy, known to historians but rediscovered and opened to the public as a museum in 2004; a few shanties that capture long-lost memories in the notorious Cabbage Patch neighborhood; and the buildings surrounding fifteen gigantic gallows frames that guard abandoned mine shafts.

This book examines demolition and preservation and the history connected with them in the nation's largest National Historic Landmark District (NHLD).

Mary MacLane provided a lyrical description of Butte in its heyday, about 1917:

> As much as for the mountains in their mourning intimateness I feel love for
> all the outsides and surfaces of the town itself…
> the stone streets full of houses and shops and stores and brick walls…
> the vacant lots where boys play ball…
> the big mines on the Hill busily working day and night…
> the Brophy grocery-window full of attractive grocery-food…
> the St. Gaudens statue of Marcus Daly…

INTRODUCTION

Ex-Senator Clark's old-fashioned closed house in Granite Street…
the stone Episcopal Church with the memorial windows…
the surprising steep Idaho Street hill…
the brilliant sparkling look of the town from far out on the Flat late in the evening, like a mammoth broken tiara of starry diamonds…

Part I

BRICK BOOMTOWN

Its insistent charm is that it goes on strongly resembling itself year after year.
—Mary MacLane in
I, Mary MacLane: A Diary of Human Days *(1917)*

S elf-preservation, rather than historic preservation, is why Butte today still holds thousands of historic properties.

Nothing remains from the early ramshackle camp that sprang up here in the 1860s only to be abandoned as the easy-to-find gold played out in the early 1870s. Log cabins and the few rough-hewn structures dotting the hill and the edges of the gulches—all are gone. But some prospectors returned to Butte in 1874 and 1875 to discover hidden gold, silver and copper in the rocks. The first hint of renewal meant that Simon Hauswirth's new Hotel de Mineral, the first hotel in the city, had customers aplenty when it was built in 1875 at the southwest corner of Broadway and Main. High-quality construction suggests that a sawmill had been established by that time, and skilled carpenters were available.

In Butte's second boom during the late 1870s, when the population jumped from a low of 61 in 1874 to 3,363 in 1880, the town looked like a relatively well-established mining camp—still rough and dirty, but with substantial wood buildings increasing in number each year.

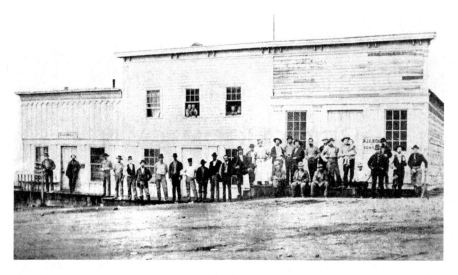

Simon Hauswirth's Hotel de Mineral, Butte's first two-story building, included a post office at left and a saloon at right. It stood at the southwest corner of Main and Broadway in 1875. *Author's collection, gift of Al Hooper.*

THE BRICK ORDINANCE

Hotel owner Simon Hauswirth was among the fledgling city's first elected aldermen, serving on the initial city council in 1879–80. Butte's first mayor, Henry Jacobs, built the oldest surviving brick house in Butte in 1879—his home, at the corner of Montana and Granite Streets. The Jacobs administration promoted brick construction to combat the fires that swept the growing community's wooden businesses and homes in the late 1870s, passing the first city ordinance regulating construction. Jacobs himself, a German Jew who fought for the South at the Siege of Vicksburg in the Civil War, exemplified the growing ethnic diversity that was beginning to create a mining metropolis.

By 1893, the ordinance governing building construction had grown to a twenty-nine-page document, specifying that "the walls and outer coverings of all buildings hereafter erected or enlarged within the fire limits of the City of Butte shall be built of stone, brick, or iron, or other incombustible materials." Outside, party and inside wall thicknesses were specified—the outside walls of a two-story building were to hold at least twenty-four inches of brick in the basement, sixteen inches on the first floor and twelve inches on the second story. No building was to be erected with less than eight-inch-thick brick walls—and that was just for one-story structures.

The 1893 revised building ordinance was enacted at a time when Butte's population was exploding tenfold, from 3,363 in 1880 to 30,470 in 1900. And census figures for Butte always reflect only the townsite itself—from the earliest days, the Butte hill was a concentration of humanity, partly adjacent to, but technically beyond, the city proper and its "fire limits."

Regulations of all sorts were enacted. Despite Butte's reputation as a wide-open town, houses of prostitution were declared by ordinance to be public nuisances in 1890, with the fine for operating them $100 per day. Exceeding six miles per hour on a bicycle could get you a $50 fine, spitting on the sidewalk cost anywhere from $1 to $100 and failure to hitch your horse resulted in a $5 penalty. But the building ordinance is by far the most detailed and extensive of all those enacted in that time of growth. The all-

The September 1905 "million dollar fire" on Park Street attracted many onlookers. *Library of Congress.*

important building ordinance was filled with specifications for penalties, ranging from $5 to $300 per day, and up to ninety days of imprisonment, depending on the violation. And owners, builders, contractors, architects, occupants and lessees could all be deemed violators. Building with brick was a serious business in 1890s Butte.

Like the rules against prostitution and gambling, the requirement for brick construction was well meant but often ineffective. Fires bedeviled Butte from its earliest days to the 1980s and beyond. Nonetheless, it is largely due to brick that so many historic buildings survive in Butte in the twenty-first century.

Brick's permanence symbolizes Butte's transition from a mining camp and ephemeral boomtown to an industrial urban community. Mining's dominance meant that Butte was never really part of the rural, cowboy West that was central to development across Montana beyond Butte. And it grew to become a metropolis, the largest city in a vast area between Minneapolis, Denver and Spokane.

Most brick in 1880s Butte was produced locally, but the high elevation and granite substrate were not the best to generate soils and clays for making the finest brick. Anaconda—lower and wetter and with more soil development—took over as the leading source Butte's brick after 1900. As the city became home to wealthier individuals, more and more brick was imported, from Helena, the eastern United States and even from overseas, but some brick was produced around Butte until 1955.

Common brick—the type used for the less prestigious buildings in Butte—has no special treatment such as glazing or additives or higher firing temperature to enhance its strength. As a result, it crumbles and deteriorates relatively easily in Butte's weather extremes. Preserving, restoring and repointing such brick is an important element of historic preservation in Butte today.

All mining communities undergo booms and busts. Butte was no exception, but it also enjoyed one of the longest sustained booms of any mining town anywhere. Butte grew without a significant break from 1875 to 1917; 30,000 people in 1895 had tripled to an estimated 100,000 in 1917. This anomalous metropolis, out of place in ranching-focused Montana, exploded in three distinct building booms.

Butte was already expanding dramatically in 1882 when Marcus Daly's miners reached the astonishingly rich four-hundred-foot-thick Anaconda copper vein. The long boom began at that time and continued into the early 1890s. The 1893 silver panic slowed, but by no means stopped, Butte's mining and construction, and by the late 1890s, many homes, from miner's cottages to middle-class frame homes and brick mini-mansions, were under construction.

The population continued to swell with new tides of immigrants from all over Europe. The second "boomlet" (1906–8) was marked by the erection of many of Butte's largest churches, often the second to stand on the same land. First Baptist (1907–8) and St. Mark's Lutheran (1906–8) are two churches built in this period. The Leonard, an upscale residential hotel, Symons's second department store, the Napton Hotel, Carpenters' Union Hall, Cass Gilbert's State Savings Bank (Metals Bank today) and the prestigious Silver Bow Club were all built in 1906.

Architecture in Butte during the final boomlet (1915–17) was, like earlier construction, dominated by brick, but building lines from this time are sharper and less ornamented than some earlier structures. The Knights of Columbus Hall and old YMCA typify this period.

1884 REVISITED

Despite the brick ordinance, Butte's Sanborn Fire Insurance map for August 1888 locates the ruins of some major fires. The original Maguire Opera House on Broadway, houses on East Copper Street and Warfield & Gwin's Livery & Feed Stable on Park all burned down in early 1888, and another major fire in 1889 destroyed the first block of Granite Street west of Main.

J.W. Beal's Centennial Hotel fell to the flames on April 24, 1888, resulting in a $56,000 loss; Jennie M. Ledden and Postmaster Frank Lincoln died in the fire. Dr. Beal, an Ohio native, had practiced medicine at Alder Gulch and German Gulch for twelve years before coming to Butte in 1876. By 1879, Beal was among eight physicians and surgeons, with one dentist, who advertised their services to Butte. In addition to his work in medicine, Beal was a politician who served in the territorial legislature and was elected Butte mayor in 1881. He built and managed the Centennial Hotel (opened on July 4, 1876) at the corner of Main and Granite where the Hennessey Building stands today.

The two-story Centennial Hotel included a saloon run by Beal's son-in-law (George Newkirk), an office, the thirty- by forty-foot dining room, kitchen, laundry, wood house and a two-level outhouse, as well as a nearby icehouse. George Newkirk's Butte mineral collection was reported to be the best in the territory and was reportedly sent for display at the Centennial

Exposition in Philadelphia. Dr. Beal died at German Gulch, where his son owned at least two mines, on June 8, 1901, at age seventy-three.

Butte's first Sanborn Fire Insurance map dates to 1884, as does a bird's-eye view plan published by J.J. Stoner. Together they provide a snapshot of 1884 life in Butte that is almost entirely gone.

THE FRONT STREET HUB

Front Street in 1884 had to be a busy hub where visitors got their first glimpse of the "Richest Hill on Earth." It was somewhat isolated from Butte proper, which stood about a mile or so up the hill. Because Main and Montana didn't reach Front Street, access was primarily via the branching extensions of Arizona and Utah, which then, as now, came down to the railroad terminal (Utah Northern in 1884).

Both sides of the railway were dominated by the Montana Lumber & Produce Company with its mill. The three-story structure included the sawmill on the first level, a sash and door factory on the second and a planing mill on the third floor. The mill even ran on Sundays and "frequently at night," with lighting provided by kerosene lanterns (no smoking was allowed). Small buildings west of huge lumber piles included the boiler, a shed where shavings were collected by blowers, the iron-clad drying room, a twelve-thousand-gallon water tank, an eighteen-foot-high thirty-thousand-gallon oil tank, paint and varnish storage and offices.

Montana Lumber's freight offices across the tracks stored sashes, doors, wagons, paints and oils in one building and hay, grain and produce in another. To the east, Kirkendall & Brown's warehouse held buggies, and continuing west on what would become Front Street was Northwestern Forwarding Company's warehouse, with hay and grain bins, across from the saloon and billiard hall.

The two-story boardinghouse, near what would become the corner of Utah and Front, was across from the Caplice, McCune & Company station, where it received and sent grain and produce to its stores in Walkerville, Butte, and elsewhere in southwest Montana. It was behind the railroad freight depot along with J.E. Richards's two-story oil warehouse and Dolman's hay and grain warehouse.

The passenger depot was conveniently located just a few steps from the Northwestern Hotel. A long low building along the tracks held coal and salt bins. A service building stood on the spur south of the main line; the spur passed the main water tank, near the small open-air circle where engines were rotated—the predecessor to the roundhouse that was eventually built near there.

THE CAPLICE BLOCK

John Caplice and his partner Alfred McCune were Utah businessmen who became active in Butte in the early 1880s. Caplice was born in County Tipperary, Ireland, in 1829 and was at Bannack in 1863. He died in 1903. In addition to the huge building at Park and Montana, the partners had a general merchandise establishment on Main Street north of Daly Street in Walkerville and several other stores around southwest Montana, and they were involved in the initial construction of the Montana Central Railroad (MCRR) in 1886. The MCRR reached Butte on November 10, 1888, and joined with the Great Northern in 1889. McCune lived for the most part in Salt Lake City, where his 1900 home is considered to be one of the finest mansions in the West.

The Caplice Block was among Butte's larger buildings in 1884. It stood at the southwest corner of Park and Montana, and it included a general

A portion of the 1884 bird's-eye view of Butte shows the developing metropolis. *Library of Congress.*

store on the north side (facing Park), with tenements above on the second and third floors. The main building was a dance hall and performance theater, with dressing rooms adjacent to the Montana Street entrance. The tenements extended above the dance hall as well. In 1888, the store was a liquor store, likely Caplice Commercial Company or its predecessor, John Caplice & Company.

A "French roof" suggests that the building was in Second Empire style, probably with an ornate upper section similar to today's Finlen Hotel. This is also suggested by the appearance on the 1884 bird's-eye view.

Sutton's New Theater occupied the Caplice Block in 1900, with an entrance on Park, although a store still occupied much of the north side. In 1916, the entire building was gone, replaced by four narrow three-story stores, all opening on Park Street. Those are gone now, too.

Early Electrification

Electricity and electric light were marvels that came early to Butte, but they brought with them the danger of fires generated by improper wiring, a threat that still dogs Butte buildings in the twenty-first century.

Butte's (and Montana's) first electric light was lit at the Alice Mine in Walkerville in November 1880, just one year after Edison developed the incandescent light bulb in 1879, and helped touch off Butte's copper boom, but it wasn't an Edison light. Competing Brush arc lights lit Butte's first mines, streets and businesses, and the Brush Electric Light & Power Company was organized in 1882 with W.A. Clark at the helm, druggist H.A. D'Acheul as vice-president, merchant M.C. Connell as secretary and J. Ross Clark as treasurer.

Butte's first electric power plant, dating to 1884, was located on East Mercury Street between Main and Wyoming—later the heart of the red-light district. The plant was located in about the middle of the block, where the Blue Range building is today, but the power plant was not along the street front but rather was set back about sixty feet from the street. Two small and presumably old cabins stood along the street north of the power plant in 1884. Banard's Ditch Flume ran across the block just south of the plant, from the corner of Main and Silver to cross Wyoming and Arizona, about halfway between Mercury and Silver, effectively defining the southern edge of built-up Butte in 1884. The power plant was located near livery stables, feed stores and lumberyards, mostly along Main south of Mercury.

Two boilers in the basement generated 120 horsepower in 1884; by 1888, the building had expanded and included four boilers, an attached residence and a small stable. A crosswalk passed over the wooden flume where it crossed Wyoming, and Wyoming Street farther south was an "open sewer." Just two years later, in May 1890, Mercury between Main and Wyoming was a nearly continuous row of dwellings, and the Butte Electric Light Works plant is labeled "to be removed" on the Sanborn map. The Blue Range building replaced the individual dwellings on Mercury in 1897, and it was occupied by "female boarding," the euphemism for brothels and cribs. The power plant was still standing behind the Blue Range but was "vacant and old." The building was gone by 1916, and a short (and short-lived) street occupied what amounted to the alley between Mercury and Silver: Radium Street.

JACKSON STREET: THE EDGE OF TOWN

In 1884, a mine stood where West Mercury and Jackson Streets intersect, heart of a residential neighborhood today. Silver Bow Mining Company's Stephens Mine had a two-story hoist engine room with a steam pump and a fifty-foot-long, one-and-a-half-inch-wide hose. Two boilers generated eighty horsepower, and there was an attached carpenter shop reached by a ladder from Jackson Street. Jackson Street marked the town's western edge, labeled "Arbitrary" on the 1884 map. A nearby blacksmith's operation was essentially located in the center of the present-day intersection, with the mine complex and shaft in Mercury Street, along the south side, just west of Jackson. The mine buildings totaled about seventy square feet, and there was also an eighty-foot-long woodpile located at what is now the northwest corner of the Jackson-Mercury intersection.

The mine was still active in 1888, exploiting the Neptune Vein, but the structures there burned down in 1890 and the mine was apparently never reopened. There are no drifts (underground mine tunnels) shown on the Butte underground mine map in this area—common enough for the earliest mines.

The Silver Bow Mining Company was involved in a far-reaching lawsuit that effectively ruled that mining (subsurface) claims trump surface ownership. It is not clear whether the mine at Mercury and Jackson figured in the case, but it was a suit between surface owners in the Butte townsite and the Silver Bow Mining Company, as reported in *Montana: Its Story and Biography* by Tom Stout (American Historical Society, 1921).

Another tidbit from this neighborhood (such as it was) is the location of the "Old Jail" centered in the block along Jackson between West Park and West Galena. The large building measured about fifty by twenty-five feet and had a fenced jail yard, two small outbuildings and a stable. The "new" jail would be the one located in the city hall that had just been erected in 1884 (today's Jail House Coffee). The jail in the basement of the second city hall (24 East Broadway) was the third jail, built and in use in 1890.

SKATING RINKS

Roller skating was the rage in the United States in the 1880s, and as usual, Butte was at the leading edge. In 1884, Butte had at least two indoor roller skating rinks. The fancy one at the northeast corner of Granite and Alaska—directly across Alaska from today's Silver Bow Club Office Building—was a huge, two-story, 170-foot-long barnlike pavilion with a cement floor. It straddled a stream coming down from near the Original Mine. The stream contained a "large amount of water in spring and winter" and went under the pavilion via stone arches. Dressing rooms and a storage shed stood outside the pavilion itself, right at the Alaska-Granite corner. At this time, Alaska Street north of Quartz, alongside today's O'Rourke Building, was not a street per se but was occupied by vegetable gardens, with a cow corral to the east.

The second skating rink was on the north side of Park Street, where the Thomas Block (Garden of Beadin', Main Stope Gallery and so on) is today. This one-story structure was about one hundred square feet and included a basement. Both skating rinks were among the first thirty-two commercial establishments in Butte to have an electric light (one each) in February 1884.

In 1888, the Park Street rink was gone, subdivided and expanded into the two-story Thomas Block of stores, including a butcher and sausage factory, a dry goods shop, a grocery, "gents furnishings" and clothing and the Justice Court. The second floor was a furniture warehouse.

The Granite Street pavilion (called Turner Hall) was being renovated in 1888, with plans to make it into an opera house. The structure had been divided into two large spaces, with smaller shops (a saloon, a grocer and a fruit store) occupying the Granite Street front. Alaska Street to the north was still unimproved, but it was becoming more like an urban street, with several dwellings and a Chinese laundry along it. The stream had been mostly filled in or covered and turned into a subsurface culvert.

In 1890, the pavilion was still standing but was divided into three large spaces: two for the Lyceum Theater and the third for a gymnasium in the north end of the building. About half of the building was still used as a skating rink in 1891; in 1900, the rear half was a livery stable. This building with its long history was torn down about 1915 as uptown Butte's last major building boom took off. The building there today dates to this era, with a major rebuild in 1947.

Butte was growing much too quickly to allocate large spaces in the central business district to skating rinks. Other rinks developed, including the ice skating rink at the corner of Montana and Front Streets.

WILLIAM OWSLEY'S LIVERY

Stables served as garages in the 1800s, and prospering Butte had plenty. In 1884, in the area bounded by Jackson, Caledonia, Arizona and Silver Streets, at least 102 stables protected an unknown number of horses and other stock.

Three large commercial livery stables stepped up Main Street, beginning with T.M. Carr's Livery & Feed at the southeast corner of Main and Mercury. Carr had carriages available, and a large fenced feed corral adjacent to the stable accommodated plenty of horses. One block north, at the southeast corner of Galena and Main, Star Livery also provided carriages. That location was more or less in Butte's Chinatown, which centered on Galena and Main in those days.

By far the largest space for a transportation provider was Owsley and Cowan's Transfer Line Stables, established in the late 1870s. This stable and office complex stood at the northeast corner of Park and Main. In 1884, this 140- by 80-foot conglomeration included an office, a two-story lodging house, a cigar store, haylofts above the stalls on the first floor and in the basement and a carriage house with a washroom and dressing rooms for drivers. The Owsley company probably also controlled the attached saloon and card room to the north. A brothel was conveniently located just to the east on Park Street.

Postcard view of the Owsley Block at the corner of Park and Main. It burned in 1973. *Author's collection.*

The livery business built William Owsley's fortune, and in 1888–91, he built the huge Owsley Block on the site of his stable complex. Owsley was born in 1842 in Independence, Missouri, and came to Montana from Idaho in 1863, part of the stampede to Bannack and Montana's first gold rush. Within a year, he had relocated to Butte and was working as a saloonkeeper, and he started his livery business in 1874.

Owsley was twice elected Butte mayor, serving terms in 1882–83 and 1884–85, probably winning a few votes in part through his campaign slogan, "Down with cheap Chinese labor." A few was all he needed: he defeated his opponent in 1884 by just 19 votes of 1,051 cast. Lee Mantle, later U.S. senator and founder of the *Inter Mountain* newspaper in Butte, was an early partner with Owsley in his livery business, as was Henry Valiton, Butte's second mayor. Valiton was also a partner in Marchesseau & Valiton, a business with a three-story store located two blocks north of Owsley's stable and known as the Beaver Block.

Multiple buildings on East Park Street bear Owsley's name, including Blocks 1 and 2 that replaced a brothel and survive today at 39–45 East Park. Both were finished by early 1891, while the much larger corner block was still under construction.

Owsley died in 1919, but his prestigious building served Butte until 1973. It housed the Butte Business College and many offices in its early days and

Owsley Block No. 2 on East Park, built in 1891 and still standing. *Photo by Jet Lowe, Library of Congress.*

was known as the Medical Arts Center when it burned down on July 28, 1973. In 1893, the Butte Business College boasted the "most elegant rooms of any business college in the Northwest," providing "thorough practical schooling for young ladies and gentlemen." Their departments filled the Owsley Block's fifth floor, and their eleven faculty members conducted classes in bookkeeping, plain and ornamental penmanship, commercial law, shorthand, typewriting, practical English and mechanical drawing. The college left the Owsley Block in 1953 but survived in Butte until 1975.

WEST BROADWAY

The south side of the first block of West Broadway includes some old buildings, but only one survives from 1884. The Independent Order of Good Templars (IOGT) Hall at 42–44 West Broadway is the only remnant from that time still standing today. (This anti-alcohol fraternal organization also admitted women.) Two doors down, the International Order of Odd Fellows (IOOF) Hall had its foundation laid by September 1884, and it's another long-term survivor in this block.

Both the IOGT and IOOF Halls witnessed the American Protective Association (APA) riot in this block on July 4, 1894. The APA was a short-lived bigoted organization—anti-Catholic, anti-Irish, anti-immigrant and anti-union, an organization likely doomed to fail in a cosmopolitan city like Butte. But for whatever reason, two saloonkeepers put the APA banner in their windows for the Independence Day holiday, and after a few sticks of dynamite were tossed into one saloon, the fighting became general. It continued for close to twelve hours and involved many hundreds of men in interconnected brawls. The militia was called; it was in Helena, and when the men reached Butte by train in midafternoon, the melee was still in progress. Special Deputy Dennis Daly, attempting to help clear the way for the militiamen, jostled the wrong guy, who pulled a gun and shot Daly dead in front of the Odd Fellows Hall.

The IOGT Hall included a stage in the basement and a dwelling on the first floor. It along with the restaurant-saloon in mid-block and the prestigious bank at the corner of Main all had slate roofs, while all the others had wooden shingles. Most buildings were "cloth lined," meaning that their frame walls were insulated only by a canvas lining. Sheetrock (gypsum wallboard omnipresent in homes and offices today) was patented in 1894 by Augustine Sackett in New York but was not in common use until 1900 and later.

Hart & Lavelle's livery stable at mid-block had a basement with stone walls on two sides, and the bank had a stone basement. The Donnell, Clark & Larabie bank occupied the first floor at the corner of Broadway and Main (where D.A. Davidson is today), with offices above and a barber and bathhouse in the basement, where they had their own large boiler. The cornice was metal, probably tin. This building lasted until 1916, and its 1916 replacement was, in turn, replaced by the building there today in the 1960s.

Robert Donnell expanded his Deer Lodge bank in 1877 with a new Butte branch, where the twenty-five- by one-hundred-foot lot at the corner of Broadway and Main cost $1,400 on April 18, 1877. Donnell's clerks, W.A. Clark and S.E. Larabie, took charge of the Butte branch and became the owners when another Donnell venture failed, in New York in 1884. Clark's fortune began in this bank when he took some mine property, including the

Travona, in lieu of loan payments, and an uninterested Larabie accepted a band of horses in exchange for his half interest in the mines. Shrewd investment, political chicanery and luck made Clark into the nation's second-richest man (after John D. Rockefeller) by the time he died in 1925, when his fortune was estimated at $200,000,000 in that era's money.

January 2012 construction work running from the parking lot at Quartz and Alaska to Broadway (in front of the IOGT Hall), Park and Galena Streets focused on a pre-1884 underground water/sewer line. Before mining and building altered the landscape, that line was a flowing stream that came down the hill from the Centerville area, about where Alaska Street is today. South of Granite to Galena, the stream had largely been converted to an underground culvert by summer 1884, but it was still a ditch or open sewer below Galena Street.

THE DESTROYING ANGEL

In about 1880, prominent Butte businessman Lee Mantle (later mayor, newspaperman, brothel owner and U.S. senator) established the Diadem Claim in the heart of Butte's growing business district, angling from the corner of Broadway and Montana southeast to Main and Galena and a bit beyond. By 1882, Mantle was seeking to evict surface owners from the Diadem Claim, but they didn't go quietly. The surface business owners banded together and, finding a possible legal flaw in the Diadem, established the Destroying Angel Claim, encompassing the Diadem. The name was deliberately chosen to reflect the expected "destruction" of Mantle's eviction attempt. And the Destroying Angel partners prevailed; Mantle's case was dismissed in 1884. But it wasn't over yet.

The partners fell on one another, in various disputes over who owed what to the Destroying Angel money pool. The cases dragged on for more than ten years and ultimately went to the Montana Supreme Court, with Chief Justice William Pemberton participating in the decision to compel one partner to pay $200 to the others. Pemberton's Butte home at 39 East Granite was just two blocks from the east end of the Destroying Angel Claim, while Lee Mantle's house on North Montana was two blocks north of the west end.

A mine was eventually developed on the Destroying Angel Claim, but it never seems to have produced much (if anything), even though its location was given as 35 West Galena (rear) from 1895 to 1910. The Destroying Angel is commemorated in the name of a whiskey made at Headframe Spirits, a boutique distiller whose building stands on the western edge of the old Destroying Angel claim.

SURVIVING 1884

An inventory and analysis conducted in 1981 listed twenty-five buildings built before 1884 that still stood in Butte. A few that certainly predate 1884 were missed, including the middle of the 100 block on North Main Street and the IOGT Hall on Broadway, and a few that were built soon after 1884 were included. The correct total in 1981 should have been about thirty-two.

A similar review for this book indicated that in 2012 Butte still contained about twenty-five pre-1884 buildings—quite remarkable given the booms, busts, fires and demolitions the city saw in the following 125 years.

Marcus Daly was the "winner" in the war of the copper kings, at least to the extent that it was his company that became the Anaconda Company. Sculptor Augustus St. Gaudens's last significant work, the 1906 statue of Marcus Daly, originally stood on North Main Street as seen here. It was moved to Park Street at the entrance to the Montana Tech campus in 1941. *Photo by Arthur Rothstein, 1939, Library of Congress.*

Brick Boomtown

The pre-1884 home where copper king Marcus Daly lived in 1885 stood at the corner of Montana and Quartz Streets, but like Daly himself, it wasn't long for Butte. Once Daly had established his smelter town Anaconda, and his dream home in Hamilton where he could raise his beloved horses, he didn't spend much time in Butte. Daly, who died in 1900, was the "winner" in the war of the copper kings, to the extent that it was his company that became the Anaconda Company. The house at Montana and Quartz, a modest two-story brick-veneered frame building, was demolished in 1910 to make way for the expanded second Silver Bow County Courthouse, which now occupies the block bounded by Granite, Montana, Quartz and Alaska.

Part II
EVERYDAY LIFE IN METROPOLITAN BUTTE

For mixture, for miscellany—variedness, Bohemianism—where is Butte's rival?
–Mary MacLane in The Story of Mary MacLane *(1902)*

Once the initial gold rush mining camp was finished by the late 1860s, the choices were to either decline to a ghost town or develop as a metropolis. Silver provided the road to survival—over time, Butte has produced more than 700 million ounces, probably ranking it third in the world for silver. But that survival in the late 1870s grew into an explosion by the early 1880s as demand for copper soared.

Copper—used to transmit electricity and telephone and telegraph signals—created the longest, most valuable mining boom in U.S. history. The wealth that resulted meant that every architectural style appeared, from mansard-roofed Second Empire and Queen Anne mansions to vernacular sheds in the Cabbage Patch, Butte's slum. The business of living in a wide-open boomtown led to juxtaposition of rich and poor, blurring class distinction, at least on streetscapes. A tiny miner's cottage might stand across the street from an elegant mansion, which was next door to a residential hotel. And that exploding population's needs were reflected in buildings.

Boardinghouses Rule:
The Florence and Finntown

The dominantly young, single, male population made for "a very bully of a city, stridently male, blusteringly profane, boisterous and boastful," according to Kinsey Howard in *Montana: High, Wide and Handsome.* By the thousand, they lived in boardinghouses.

What was a boardinghouse? It could be a small, simple home, perhaps run by a widow whose husband had died in a mine fire. The widow would take in a handful of boarders to make ends meet, if her house were large enough. It might be a two-story or taller building erected specifically to serve as accommodations, with any number of single rooms together with a dining hall. It might be a huge hotel-like block, three, four or five stories high. The key difference between a boardinghouse and furnished rooms, apartments, flats, sleeping rooms and the like was *boarding*—meals were available.

The Braund boardinghouse shortly after the 1921 fire. *Photograph courtesy of the World Museum of Mining.* © *World Museum of Mining.*

The Braund House, at 1302–1308 East Talbot (later renamed East Mercury) at the corner of Watson Avenue, dominated the industrial side on the far east. It stood between the Dutton and Monitor Mines, with the Adams Shaft across the street and the Great Northern railroad's main line crossing ninety feet away. It was erected as a relatively small two-story boardinghouse in about 1890, but within ten years, it had added an annex to more than double its size. After the expansion, rates for room and board ran $1.00 to $1.50 per day. In 1916, a third story was added, the dining room measured about thirty-two square feet and the saloon included a large dance hall. The eighty-five-room Braund was torn down shortly after two "mysterious" fires on April 23, 1921, to be replaced by a beer warehouse. Today Talbot, Watson and other nearby streets are gone, swallowed by the southern edge of the Berkeley Pit.

The great-grandmother of all the boardinghouses was the Florence Hotel. Built in 1898 at the behest of and with financing by Amalgamated (Anaconda) Company officers, it replaced the Hale House, which burned down on March 21, 1898. It stood on East Broadway, at the southwest corner of Thornton Avenue—the street that today seems like an alley on the east side of the Broadway Café.

The huge new edifice was constructed in three sections, totaling 110 feet of exposure on Broadway and extending 140 feet to the south. With three stories and a basement on the north side and four stories and a basement on the south, it had two 12- by 80-foot light wells, even though it also had electric lights. To guard against continual fire hazards, each floor had a 200-foot-long, one-and-a-half-inch-wide hose, and the double boiler and the bake house were both enclosed in brick, with brick ceilings and an iron-clad door connecting with the hotel. The boilers supplied steam heat to the rooms; the bake house and a separate 12-foot-wide oven operated throughout the day to serve as many as four hundred diners at each sitting—three hundred hotel residents and another one hundred from elsewhere. The dining hall took up almost the entire eastern third of the building on the first floor (the bar occupied that section at the Broadway Street front, and a small barbershop also served customers there). In the washroom, 130 men at a time could clean up. The Florence was *big*.

In its early years, the Florence had problems with management and inefficient operations. John Ryan, Anaconda Copper Mining Company president (his mansion stands at 105 North Excelsior Street), asked saloonkeeper Hugh O'Daly to take over. O'Daly owned Daly's Place, a bar at 106 North Main Street where his innovations, including replacing the original twenty-five-foot bar with a seventy-five-foot one, had turned his establishment into the "most popular bar in Montana" by 1905. With that success under his belt, O'Daly bought the Florence in 1906. The previous operators, Mr. and Mrs. Chad Flood, had only 150 guests in three hundred rooms when O'Daly took over; he paid $3,500, down from the Floods' asking price of $5,000. Strictly speaking, the Anaconda Company owned the property, and O'Daly owned the business, but for practical purposes, the place was O'Daly's.

O'Daly immediately employed the principle of spending money to make money. He bought six hundred new mattresses (putting two single beds in each room), installed a new bar and bought new dishes for the dining room. His most controversial move may have been increasing wages: chambermaids and waitresses made $30/month for a twelve-hour shift, but O'Daly upped it to $35 a month for eight hours a day. The cook went from $125/month to $150, and there were raises for other employees, including butchers, bakers, bartenders and clerks. Within one week, he was at 100 percent occupancy. Other hoteliers and lodging businesses grumbled, but his success was inarguable. The unions' ascendancy at the same time—miners got the eight-hour day in Butte in 1900–1906 as well—likely enhanced his favor with his guests, virtually all of whom were miners.

The Florence sat squarely within Finntown, which centered on East Granite, Broadway and Park and extended several blocks east from the Florence. But the Florence was almost entirely Irish, from O'Daly down to Donegal-born maid Annie O'Byrne, who worked there for thirteen years; 85 percent of the guests were Irish.

O'Daly's refurbishing of the Florence cost him $11,748, a princely sum in 1906, but in the first year, he turned a $23,000 profit. The Florence quickly became known as the "Big Ship," not for the size of the place, huge though it was, but because it was said that on a weekend, enough liquor was consumed there to float "a mighty big ship."

Guests at the Florence paid $8.00 to $12.00 per week for their bed and board—not counting what they spent in the Big Ship's saloon. Mary Buckley's much smaller boardinghouse at 526 North Wyoming (in Corktown, as Mary was from Macroom, County Cork) housed seventeen residents and fed thirty more in 1914 at $7.00 per week for three meals and $8.00 a week for three meals and lodging—all at a time when miners earned $3.50 per day.

The Big Ship's business importance was not lost on Centennial Brewing president Henry Mueller. In August 1907, less than a year into O'Daly's ownership of the Florence, Mueller told O'Daly that Daly's Place was his best customer and the Florence was second best. To maintain that relationship, Mueller offered O'Daly 2,500 shares in Centennial valued at $5,000. O'Daly received a $175 monthly dividend from 1907 to 1919 and thought it his best investment—that was more than double a well-paid miner's monthly wage during most of that time. Prohibition affected the breweries in Butte, of course, and the mothballed Centennial burned down just as prohibition was about to be repealed in 1933. O'Daly recalled that the insurance premium was unpaid, a week past due—his investment immediately became worthless. O'Daly also thought, "Prohibition was the most dasterly [*sic*] law ever passed."

With his profits in 1907, O'Daly started a library at Lisdoonan School in his native Ireland, where he learned to read and write. The school he attended had no books because the landlord had confiscated them in 1853. His donations continued until the troubles began and the Sinn Fein movement got going. Father O'Connor ran the Lisdoonan but was "of the Parliamentary School" and rejected O'Daly's donation for a prize for the best essay on freeing Ireland. O'Connor sent the money back and closed the library.

With the October 7, 1907 financial crash and panic, Anaconda layoffs and general hard times began, and the Florence was quickly down to fifty guests. O'Daly closed the hotel and went to New Mexico but returned and reopened the following March. By 1911, O'Daly was losing interest in the Florence, and he sold it and bought the resort at Gregson Hot Springs. He

Typical boardinghouse interior. *Photo by Jet Lowe, Library of Congress.*

continued to visit Butte and support Irish freedom; he met Éamon de Valera on his Butte tour in 1921.

Soon after O'Daly's departure, the Florence began to go downhill. In 1911–12, a study of sanitary conditions in Butte described the Florence as having "[r]ooms fairly clean, but toilets very bad; eight toilets in basement very dark and dirty. Rear of this hotel, in alley, very dirty and insanitary. Slops and refuse thrown into shed in rear." At least one tuberculosis case was noted in January 1912, and the dining room at the Florence had air that tested positive for tetanus.

Hugh O'Daly died in about 1946, and the Florence was torn down about the same time. The lot was filled by tiny little row houses in about 1951, but they are gone now, too, and the site at 246–250 East Broadway is a vacant lot, sometimes used to stage performances during the Montana Folk Festival.

Like the Florence, almost all of the Finntown neighborhood is gone. Boardinghouses and lodging houses operated by Finns served miners of

Congested housing in Finntown. This is probably East Granite Street. *Butte–Silver Bow Public Archives.*

all nationalities. On East Broadway, the 300 block alone held six two-story duplexes and lodging houses, three three-story blocks, one five-plex and one six-plex. In the 400 block, sixteen two-story lodgings, one three-story and one six-plex were available. Just three single-family homes (which might have had boarders) occupied the 500 block, along with thirteen two-story and one three-story boarding and lodging houses. All are gone today, except for the Helsinki Bar at 402 East Broadway, which started out as a bay-fronted store and home with boarding in the basement and on the second floor. East Broadway was ground zero for the Berkeley Pit expansion, and even though the pit did not grow to the west as expected, the nearby neighborhoods were lost nonetheless.

Finnish boardinghouses and other establishments were located near the mines just a fraction of a mile up Anaconda Road. Saunas added extra value to miners beyond the required saloons and excellent fifty-cent meals. In addition to highly valued skills as timbermen—you wanted your mine shaft to be framed by Finns—the Finns brought with them some of the most radical socialism in the early twentieth century. The Finlander Hall on North Wyoming, two blocks below Mary Buckley's house in Corktown,

"Steam Baths" on the tall black standpipe refers to saunas in Finntown. The location is the 500 block of East Broadway, with the Moonlight Mine behind at left. *Photo by Arthur Rothstein, 1939, Library of Congress.*

stood at the western edge of Finntown as a gymnasium and social center for the three or four thousand Finns in Butte, but it became a political center as well.

Finlander Hall was the focal point for agents and officers of the Industrial Workers of the World (the IWW, or "wobblies"). On June 8, 1917, a fire at the Granite Mountain and Speculator Mines killed 168 miners, the deadliest hard-rock mine disaster in the United States before or since. The strike that followed was winding down in July when IWW leader Frank Little came to Butte. He gave incendiary speeches around town, attended meetings in the Finlander Hall and spent his nights next door at Mrs. Byrnes's boardinghouse—that is, until the early morning hours of August 1, when armed thugs, likely sent by the Anaconda Company, hauled him from his bed and lynched him. His brutal death sent shock waves through the labor movement nationally and was front-page news in Berkeley, California, for a week.

When the decision was made to "bury Frank Little on the fighting ground" of Butte, his funeral procession became the largest ever seen in Butte, with at least 2,500 marching with his coffin through town and an estimated 12,000 people lining the streets. Frank Little's grave at Mountain View Cemetery is a destination today for visitors connected to the labor movement; they come from England, France, Germany and elsewhere, knowing nothing about Butte except that Little is buried there. The company's control was such that no arrests were ever made in Little's murder.

A year later, a coordinated raid on the IWW focused on the Finlander Hall and the former St. Paul's Church at Galena and Idaho, where a U.S. Army contingent led by Captain Omar Bradley, later second in command under Dwight Eisenhower in the European Theater of World War II, disrupted the anti-Anaconda operations of the *Butte Daily Bulletin* newspaper. The *Bulletin* was nearly the only newspaper in Montana to speak against the company, and in the midst of hyperpatriotism during World War I, being anti-Anaconda was akin to being unpatriotic. The Montana Council of Defense—twelve men who effectively embodied legislative, executive and judicial power in the state—issued Order No. 12 on August 12, 1918: "No new newspapers will be created in the state; weekly newspapers are prohibited from becoming dailies." This was aimed squarely at the weekly *Butte Strike Bulletin*, which promptly became the *Butte Daily Bulletin* on August 20.

The council found a pretext to arrest publisher William F. Dunne in a nationwide IWW strike on September 13. That night, Butte police (effectively an arm of the Anaconda Company) and federal troops under

Everyday Life in Metropolitan Butte

Intersection of East Quartz and North Wyoming. The Finlander Hall and Mrs. Byrnes's boardinghouse are in the middle of the block left of the intersection. *Photograph courtesy of the World Museum of Mining.* © *World Museum of Mining.*

Captain Bradley's command raided the Finlander Hall and the church, where the *Butte Bulletin* was printed. "Loyalty officials" arrested seventy-four men and mopped up "strongholds of I.W.W. labor agitation and military 'slackness,'" as the Finlander and old church were characterized by the *Butte Miner* on September 14, 1918.

The men were charged with sedition, but most were released in the absence of clear evidence—except Bill Dunne. Despite Dunne's radicalism (or because of it), Butte's socialist-leaning people elected him to the state legislature six weeks after his arrest during the raid on the *Butte Bulletin*. His trial played out while he was serving in the statehouse, and although he was convicted, the Montana Supreme Court overturned the decision. He became a founding member of the American Communist party in 1919, and Dunne was in Moscow for the 1924–25 Communist International (Comintern) meetings. He became editor for the *Daily Worker*, the American Communist Party's newspaper, later in 1925.

St. Paul's Methodist Episcopal Church at Idaho and Galena survives in 2012, vacant, with a developer working slowly to save it. Built in 1899, it served as a church for less than twenty years. In 1918, it was owned by Larry Duggan, undertaker and later Silver Bow county sheriff. He sympathized with the radical labor cause and allowed IWW newsmen to print the *Butte Strike Bulletin* in the building, which was referred to as "Larry Duggan's Church." In subsequent years, the building held Duggan's Mortuary and Beverly Hayes' Bridal Shop.

The Finlander Hall, Mrs. Byrnes's boardinghouse and the other buildings on North Wyoming Street between Quartz and Copper were demolished in 1941, and today this stretch is the parking lot north of the Capri Motel. The two homes on North Wyoming's west side are among about twenty-five buildings left in town that were constructed before 1884. Farther north, Mary Buckley's boardinghouse is also gone, but three pre-1900 homes south of it still stand at 518, 520 and 522 North Wyoming.

Labor Violence Begins: The Union Hall

Frank Little's murder and the raids at the Finlander Hall came near the midpoint of exceptional labor unrest spanning six years. The roots of that unrest go back decades, but the 1914 dynamiting of the Miner's Union Hall touched off the worst troubles.

In 1914, Butte miners earned $3.50 per day, close to the highest pay for labor anywhere in the United States. And although that rate was for an eight-hour shift (the twelve-hour shift for the same pay disappeared about 1904–6), the rate had not changed since 1878 (except for short-term fluctuations) even though copper's price had more than doubled. Radical labor organizations such as the IWW agitated for higher wages and better working conditions—standard union demands—but also advocated the complete overthrow of the capitalist system. Factions within the Miner's Union ranged from pure IWW to pro-Anaconda.

The confrontation between the factions came to a head in June 1914 at the annual Miner's Union Day parade on the thirteenth. A riot, probably fomented by IWW men, carried a mob from the parade on Park Street up Main to the Miner's Union Hall, where they ransacked the place. Acting mayor Frank Curran, calling for calm, was pushed out the second-floor window to his death. The mob hauled the union's safe away and blew it up, finding a reported $1,500 or so.

The Miner's Union Hall in the aftermath of its dynamiting in 1914. The building at far right is James Murray's bank; Murray was the primary financial backer of Maguire's Grand Opera House. *Butte–Silver Bow Public Archives.*

Tensions were unabated over the next ten days, and on June 23 at the regular union meeting, gunshots frightened the gun-shy participants from the building. Men went a few blocks up the hill to the Steward Mine to get dynamite, and that night blast after blast—twenty-six altogether—shook uptown Butte as the union hall was destroyed.

The building was blasted, and so was the union. Two miners' unions emerged representing the diverse factions, and without a truly united workers' front, Anaconda quickly seized the opportunity to "divide and conquer," pitting one union against another. Butte was almost too unionized for its own good, with at least thirty-four different unions in the late 1910s. The IWW vision of "One Big Union" was not dead, but it had been dealt a mortal blow.

The Miner's Union Hall that stood in the 300 block of North Main Street was the second at that location. Montana's first labor organization, the Butte Workingmen's Union, was created on June 13, 1878, when miners went on strike to protest a wage cut from $3.50 to $3.00 a day at the Alice and Lexington Mines. Within three years they were erecting a union hall on North Main, but when it was nearly complete, on February 5, 1882, the structure collapsed; the specific cause was unknown but it was put down to poor construction. "This magnificent building is falling to the ground," the *Butte Miner* lamented; the $12,000 loss devastated the union coffers.

Organizers immediately solicited donations to rebuild, and a benefit performance that April at the Renshaw Opera House on Park Street was a great success. Gordon's Comique Troupe included gymnasts, short plays and skits, band productions, song and dance numbers and singing by "the Beautiful Balladist," Miss May Raymond. By 1885, a new Miner's Union Hall was in place, serving the nation's largest union local, Miner's Union #1, with 1,800 members.

After the 1914 destruction, the Miner's Union moved to temporary quarters in the upstairs room at 219 North Main, and the ruins of the old hall were demolished in 1919. Ironically, in the 1950s, the union moved its headquarters to the prestigious Silver Bow Club on Granite Street, erected in 1906 as the beautiful high-end social hall for Butte's wealthy, including the mine owners and capitalists whom the union fought against.

A memorial built in the 1990s, designed as a fallen wall, now marks the site of the 1914 dynamiting, just a block west of North Wyoming where the Finlander Hall once stood.

LAUNDRIES AND MOLLIE WALSH

As Butte grew from a mining camp to a huge industrial metropolitan city, amenities grew to accommodate the needs and wants of a population with money to spend. Laundries popped up all over town, mostly operated by Chinese citizens, but with improved technologies, growing population and prejudice against the Oriental community, both household laundries and large commercial operations thrived in Butte under white management.

In 1884, Butte had nine Chinese laundries. The first non-Chinese commercial laundry appears to have been the Butte Steam Laundry, on West Granite in 1885, across from the skating rink pavilion at Alaska Street. They competed with twenty-one Chinese laundries then, more than double the number from the previous year. Throughout the 1890s, the Chinese operated eighteen to thirty-one laundries, with a low of fourteen in 1896, the year white businessmen attempted a boycott of Chinese laundries. Chinese businessmen successfully brought suit against the boycott instigators, though they never saw a dime of settlement money, and some Chinese operations were curtailed for that year.

The principal non-Chinese commercial laundries in the 1890s were the Troy Steam Laundry at 51 West Mercury (later at 232 South Main), Union

The former Troy and Union Steam Laundry on West Mercury Street was the Montana Steam Laundry from 1901 to 1911. It employed as many as sixty-five people, including drivers for eight delivery wagons. The building was used in various ways—grocery wholesale, auto repairs and print shop—until it was torn down in about 1981. *Butte–Silver Bow Public Archives.*

Steam (replacing Troy on West Mercury) and the COD on East Park Street. Butte's population went from twenty-three thousand in 1890 to forty-eight thousand in 1900 as miners, prostitutes, bankers, bakers and laundry workers flocked to the thriving, growing city—to make their fortunes or perhaps just to get a job.

Eighteen-year-old Mollie Walsh came to Butte from St. Paul, Minnesota, in November 1890. Her mother was a laundress in St. Paul, and Mollie had probably picked up laundry skills from her. Only the bare bones of her Butte life are known: possibly living in Anaconda initially but doing well enough to pose for a professional photographer in Butte in 1894. She would have been doing well to earn seventy-five cents per day working twelve-hour shifts. She was working as a marker at Wason & Peet's Laundry (part of the Troy establishment on West Mercury) by 1895, when she was boarding at 69 West Broadway—a small boardinghouse sandwiched between massive business blocks on one of Butte's most prominent commercial streets. Mollie

Schultz, PALAIS STUDIO, 1894. Butte, Mont.

Mollie Walsh in Butte, age about twenty-three. *Author's collection, gift of Cindi Shaw.*

became a checker and went with Troy Laundry when it moved to South Main in 1896, and she began to room at 128 West Granite (then on the corner of Montana Street). In 1897, she was rooming at the Troy Laundry itself, and at about that time, the Salvation Army established itself next door to the Troy.

Mollie was lost to Butte after 1897 but not to history. She left in June 1897 to join the Klondike gold rush, apparently traveling with a Presbyterian minister. Mollie became well known in Skagway as a waitress and was active in the early Union church there. Alone, she established and ran a grub hut thirty miles up the White Pass Trail, likely saving the lives of hundreds if not thousands of prospectors heading for the Yukon. She married Mike Bartlett, but as the gold dwindled, so did Mike's luck. In 1902, Mollie fled their home in Dawson for Seattle, where Mike found her and shot her in the back. In 1930, another suitor, Jack Newman, dedicated a bust of Mollie in the Skagway park that bears her name, and today the "Angel of the White Pass Trail" is among the most treasured characters in Skagway's history.

All the locations in Butte associated with Mollie are gone save one. The building that housed William Schultz's Palais Studio, upstairs at 122 North Main, is vacant but still standing. All the early laundries—Chinese, white and commercial—are gone, and most are vacant lots. The last Chinese laundry in Butte, Quong Sun's shop at 329 South Arizona, was closed in 1968. Materials from the Quong Fong laundry, up the street at 110 South Arizona, are displayed at the World Museum of Mining.

THE OPERA HOUSE SAGA

Butte's cosmopolitan audiences, from miner to copper king, demanded and got the best entertainment money could buy, rivaling any performance in San Francisco, New York or Philadelphia. For nearly three decades, the most important venue for actors, orators and entertainers of all sorts was the Grand Opera House run by John Maguire.

Maguire hailed from Buttevant, County Cork, Ireland. In 1861, when he was twenty-one years old, he began his American theatrical career in San Francisco. He performed in Australia before returning to the U.S. West Coast and made his way to Butte as its second boom was beginning in 1875 to give the first recorded theatrical performance in the mining town. He returned to Butte several times in succeeding years, acting in long-gone candlelit halls where nail kegs and planks made benches for the patrons. One 1876 performance, in a two-story log building at the corner of Broadway and Main Streets, was the site that became Butte's first skyscraper, the 1901 Hirbour Tower.

The building at Broadway and Main that preceded the Hirbour Tower, probably the second skyscraper west of Minneapolis and St. Louis, had its own checkered history. It was known as "the house that Jack built" for Jack Hemple, who cut trees on the lower slopes of Mount Powell to construct this building in Deer Lodge in 1871. With Butte's fortunes growing, M.M. Charpender bought the building cheaply in Deer Lodge in 1875, dismantled it and hauled it to Butte on wagons to rebuild it on an important commercial corner. The first floor began as a saloon, and upstairs became the first Masonic Hall in Butte and reportedly also the site of Butte's first wedding ceremony. William Clark had a safe there and conducted banking operations before he had his own building.

Over its twenty-six years in Butte, the building was occupied by a saloon, restaurant, gambling house, grocery, clothing store, notions vender, cigar and confectionery shop and offices. In 1901, when it was about to come down to make room for the Hirbour Tower, the photographer Dusseau occupied most of the second floor and shared the building with Pullman's Refreshment Booth, the Shields Newsstand, Murphy's Barber Shop and Reed's Cab Company, according to the *Anaconda Standard* (May 12, 1901).

John Maguire was living permanently in Butte by about 1880, making a successful living as an entertainer and theater manager. Maguire's own Grand Opera House, at 50 West Broadway, was built in 1884–85 and was touted as the finest theater in the west beyond San Francisco. Fire destroyed that building on July 23, 1888, but with three years of sold-out house receipts behind him and abundant financial backing based on his successful track record, Maguire had a new structure erected that opened on February 28, 1889, with seats for 1,100—all filled for opening night's *A Celebrated Cause*, starring Rose Osborne. During reconstruction, Butte was not without theater: Maguire used the 170-foot-long skating pavilion that stood at the

Sarah Bernhardt, circa 1896. *Library of Congress.*

northeast corner of Granite and Alaska and called it the Lyceum. Sarah Bernhardt performed there in *Camille* on a visit when she dined with copper king William Clark at his mansion two blocks to the west.

When Sarah Bernhardt came back to Butte in September 1891 to perform *Theodora* (in French), one seat sold at auction for $75.00—a huge sum at a time when miners, well-paid though they were, earned $3.50 a day. Maguire paid $3,000.00 for Bernhardt's one-night stand and took in $5,000.00. Success seemed certain, as the thriving townsfolk had disposable income for even high-priced entertainments. Renovation in 1891 added three balconies to the Broadway Street façade, and Maguire expanded his operations to Great Falls, Anaconda and elsewhere, but Butte was always the centerpiece for Montana theater in those days. Mark Twain appeared at Maguire's in August 1895, another star among the long list of 1890s luminaries.

Copper Camp, the Depression-era collection of lusty stories of Butte, reports that Maguire's Opera House was known in 1896 and 1897 as the Murray Opera House, "in gratitude for financial backing given by Banker James A. Murray." Contemporary newspapers paint a rather more confrontational picture of ongoing financial squabbles that nearly resulted in dismantling the building.

Maguire owned the land where the new opera house stood, but in essence the bank owned the building. Or so banker James Murray claimed in 1896 when a simmering dispute boiled over. The argument concerned the rights to manage the opera company's finances and set its policies. The 1893 silver crisis affected Butte's mines and finances, perhaps including receipts and loan payments at the opera house. Nonetheless, Butte residents were shocked to read the announcement in late September 1896 that the opera house was to be torn down. Murray's men began the promised demolition by removing seats and other fixtures, taking them to vacant lots and warehouses around town. Maguire, who managed the company, promptly called Murray's supposed bluff by moving performances to the Free Public Library Auditorium, just a few doors to the west at the corner of Broadway and Academy (today's Dakota Street). The squabble began to focus on what "fixtures" were; ultimately, the courts decided that seats and such were fixtures, part of the building itself, so Murray as building owner had the right to them.

The saga played out day by day. As some windows were removed, the *Butte Miner* on October 3 wryly opined in its daily editorial that "Butte now boasts the best ventilated opera house in the U.S. Purer air never filled an auditorium or kissed the dimpled cherubs in a proscenium arch."

By October 10, with several days passing when the building's walls might or might not come down—crews stood ready to demolish—an agreement was finally reached among Maguire, Murray and their investors. Murray ended up with controlling interest in the opera company, and Maguire remained the manager. Legal proceedings continued for years, but evidently Murray and Maguire patched things up on a personal level, because when Maguire died and was buried in Monterey, California, in 1907, Murray paid for a grave marker, a huge granite block carved to portray the proscenium arch of Maguire's Butte Grand Opera House.

While the opera house investors were embroiled in their fight, another theatrical manager arrived on the Butte scene. Richard "Uncle Dick" Sutton brought *Uncle Tom's Cabin* to Butte in October 1896. By November of that year, he was operating in the three-story Caplice Block, built before 1884 at the southwest corner of Park and Montana Streets. He christened it the Union Family Theater, and it had a capacity of one thousand.

Richard "Uncle Dick" Sutton, with cane, in front of the Grand Opera House on West Broadway, circa 1908. *Butte–Silver Bow Public Archives.*

Sutton's success meant more and newer theaters. His Broadway Theater opened in September 1901 at Broadway and Montana, seating 2,175—reputedly the largest-capacity theater west of Chicago. It eventually became the Montana Theater. Kentucky-born Sutton dominated theater in Butte throughout the first quarter of the twentieth century, eventually owning most of the performing houses. He acquired Maguire's Grand Opera House about 1908, renaming it the Orpheum, the Majestic (1910–11) and, finally, the Empress (1912). It was at the Majestic that Charlie Chaplin performed on April 15, 1911, in Fred Karmo's *A Night in an English Music Hall* on his first American tour, a day before Chaplin's twenty-second birthday—his first of four visits to the Mining City.

Charlie Chaplin playing the cello, circa 1915. *Library of Congress.*

The twenty-three-year-old opera house burned down on May 25, 1912. Sutton simply moved the scheduled performances across the street to his Orion Theater, built as the Lulu in about 1908 and named for Sutton's daughter. It became the Empress immediately after the old Empress, the old Maguire Grand Opera House, burned down. Butte saw Chaplin's second visit to the Mining City when he performed at this second Empress Theater, on the north side of the 100 block of West Broadway, in December 1912.

All these theaters are gone, along with the American, the Orpheum Vaudeville, the New Empire, the Ansonia, the Rialto and others. The building that housed the Liberty Theater beginning in 1916 still stands on East Broadway, occupied by the Piccadilly Transportation Museum today. The Grand Opera House was replaced by today's Leggat Hotel in 1914; the Broadway (Montana) Theater was demolished in 1988, and the Rialto, where the first talking movies were shown in Montana, was torn down in 1965 to make way for the US Bank at the corner of Park and Main Streets. The

Demolition in 1935 of the second Empress Theater, where Charlie Chaplin performed in 1912. *Butte–Silver Bow Public Archives.*

Empress, site of Charlie Chaplin's December 1912 performance, burned in 1931 and was ultimately demolished in 1935 to become the staging area for the Greyhound Bus Station, and today the site holds a parking structure. James Murray's 1890 bank building still stands at the northwest corner of Copper and Main Streets.

Butte's dwindling population simply could not support the huge theaters of its heyday. Sutton's Broadway, later named the Montana, underwent major renovation in 1917 to create the "finest in the west," according to the *Butte Miner*, but the stage that had seen a live production of *Ben Hur* (complete with chariot race) and performances by Anna Pavlova and Al Jolson stood empty and idle fifty years later. Although its elegance once compared to that of Carnegie Hall, the Montana remained in a state of "crumbling limbo," according to Andrea McCormick in the *Montana Standard* on April 23, 1978, until all options had expired and it was finally demolished in January 1988.

The demolition of the Montana Theater, the second to last of Butte's prestigious historic theaters, did have one positive outcome. It stimulated

Broadway Theater, later the Montana Theater, at corner of Broadway and Montana. Demolished in 1988. *Photo by Jet Lowe, Library of Congress.*

Butte attorney Earl Genzberger and philanthropists Bob and Pauline Poore to work toward renovating—and saving—the last historic theater in Butte. The 1923–24 Masonic Temple auditorium annex on West Park Street—at times known as the Temple Theater, the Fox Theater and the Bow Theater—was deteriorating when the Poores and Helen Guthrie "Gus" Miller established the Butte Center for the Performing Arts to oversee its renovation. Today, the building houses the 1,200-seat Art Deco Mother Lode Theater and the Orphan Girl Children's Theater. The Butte Symphony and other groups also call the theater their home.

Twenty years of unaddressed decay at the Montana Theater also pushed the local government toward a community decay ordinance, intended to legally prevent owners from allowing their historic buildings to fall into disrepair. That rule was enforced sporadically over the following decades, with some successes and some failures. Even in 2012, the local government and preservationists continued to wrestle with the concept of "demolition by neglect" and how to make it serve the community—as well as whether that was possible in the absence of significant underpinning financial resources.

BUSTLING PARK STREET: THE THOMAS BLOCK

If Broadway was the heart of the Theater District and Main Street was noted for saloon after saloon stepping up the hill, Park Street was and is the core of uptown Butte's central business district. Clear boundaries do not exist; there were theaters on Park, stores of all sorts on Broadway and saloons everywhere, but Park Street has always had a vital business aspect, together with offices housing professionals from dentists to spiritual mediums, all filling demands from an exploding, eclectic and generally well-funded population.

Reverend Hazel Earle practiced as a spiritual medium in her office at 47 West Park, the Thomas Block, in 1901. She was an ordained minister, at least as far as the First Spiritual Progressive National Association of Utah was concerned (it gave her a diploma), and she was legally allowed to perform marriages and funerals. Her effort led to "no less than twenty-seven professional men, including lawyers and physicians" being converted to a belief in spiritual phenomena.

Reverend Earle reportedly pegged the time of Queen Victoria's death in 1901 to within seventy-five minutes, two years before the fact. She conducted public meetings Sunday and Wednesday evenings, apparently including "life readings that would satisfy the most skeptical."

Earle held forth upstairs at the Thomas Block, the former roller skating rink; she also conducted large public evening sessions a few doors west, in room 36 at the Washington Block, which is gone today. Hazel Earle lived at 201 East Granite Street, the Jacobs House, on the corner opposite the courthouse. Among her seven local competitors was Madam Zazell, a clairvoyant and palmist who also reportedly assisted with mining exploration—she was "positively unexcelled and more than a few individuals have acquired large fortunes through following her advice."

Earle practiced in Salt Lake City (258 Main Street, room 2) in the summer of 1898 before coming to Butte. Uncertain records suggest that she was from Fayette, Iowa, and that she died in 1923. Despite her powers, she was in Butte about a year, listed only in the city directory for 1901.

The original Thomas Block burned down on September 1, 1912 in one of the costliest conflagrations in Butte's first seventy-five years, with losses estimated at nearly $221,000 in the dollars of the day. In addition to the building itself, businesses such as Oechsli's Furniture Company, Everybody's Shoes, Harry Krueger Cigars, Pallas Candy and banks in and near the block suffered losses. The Miner's Savings Bank was burned out but announced

Original Thomas Block, with Lutey's first grocery store, circa 1908. Note the granite-paved street with concrete crosswalk. The six-story building in the distance is the Clark Hotel, destroyed by the Penney's fire in 1972. *From a stereopticon view, courtesy Bob McMurray, Old Butte Historical Adventures.*

no need for concern by depositors since "the vault is standing. The safe is secure and will be opened as soon as it has cooled off sufficiently," according to the September 2, 1912 *Anaconda Standard*. The American Theater, not fifty feet down the block to the east, bragged that thanks to its "fire proof and practically non-destructible building," its sell-out audience enjoyed one of the season's best shows the evening of the day the Thomas Block was destroyed. Fire Chief Pete Sanger was certain that the disaster was the work of a "firebug," but no arrest was made.

Another 1912 fire exceeded even the huge cost of the Thomas Block fire. On April 10, 1912, a cigarette tossed into a hay bin at Campana Feed Company's warehouse at Iron and Nevada Streets quickly spread to consume two entire blocks, from Aluminum to Iron and Nevada to Utah Street. Although this was on the edge of the warehouse district, many homes and boardinghouses occupied those blocks in 1912. At least two hundred people were made homeless, and the financial loss was estimated at $350,000 at the time, later revised downward to $295,000.

The Olsen Block, a two-story rooming house at 741–747 South Wyoming, was destroyed. As reported by the *Anaconda Standard* on April 11, 1912: "A solid wall of fire crashed in windows. Sleeping roomers, many of them railroad men just off shift, fled in terror. A 200-foot runway furnished an opening for the flames and in 10 minutes the scene was one of terror. Nearly 100 roomers, some clad only in nightrobes, ran in a panic just as the rear wall caved in."

National Hotel (at left) on Utah Street. *Photo by Jet Lowe, Library of Congress.*

The National Hotel on Utah Street was threatened, but a change in the wind and four hours of firefighting saved it. The National survived until August 2010, when it was consumed by an arson fire allegedly set by two residents.

The Thomas Block was rebuilt in 1913 to the design of prominent Butte architect Herman Kemna for developer Adolph Pincus. Pincus told the *Butte Miner* of July 30, 1913, "I am a firm believer in the future of Butte, and the fact that I am investing $75,000 in the new Thomas Block is very certain that I look to see this city keep right on growing and advancing. Butte is getting better every year, and this is going to be the best business year the city has ever had." In 2012, shops and art galleries occupy the block.

EVERYDAY LIFE AT THE LOCAL BAR

It's a historical fact that everyday life in Butte centered on saloons. Butte today still has the not-too-positive reputation as a hard-drinking town, but it can be nothing like it once was. Even after prohibition, and in the face of depression-borne population decline in 1936, Butte police chief Walter Shay reportedly characterized the town as "an island of easy money, entirely surrounded by whiskey." But at its peak in 1917, Butte had some 240 named saloons, mostly in the uptown central business district.

It was to the uptown that reformer Carrie A. Nation marched in January 1910, hatchet in hand. By the time she reached the red-light district at Arizona and Mercury Streets, she had hundreds in the crowd with her, but it would be a mistake to think that they followed her cause. The "jeering crowd of rowdies and curiosity

Carrie Nation, circa 1909. *Library of Congress.*

seekers," as the *Butte Miner* characterized them, were probably looking for free entertainment on a cold winter night, and they got it.

At the ABC saloon/brothel/dance hall at the corner of Mercury and Wyoming, Mrs. Nation reviled the patrons but was sent out with the orchestra playing "What the Hell Do We Care." A block to the east, at the high-end Windsor Parlor House, she was forcibly ejected by May Malloy, the madam, who ripped the sixty-three-year-old Nation's bonnet from her head and "for good measure in parting administered a kick."

Despite the signs in all saloons declaring "All Nations Welcome Except Carrie," the reformer seemed to be undaunted by Butte. She even called out Mayor Nevin as a saloonkeeper, comparing him to a wolf in charge of a flock of chickens.

During her three-day visit, Carrie Nation spoke to her admirers in Butte at various churches, including Grace Methodist Episcopal, Shortridge Christian Church across from St. Patrick's on Mercury and Mountain View Methodist at Quartz and Montana. Eclectic, diverse Butte was not entirely unified in its opposition to temperance; the churches were packed, and she did a "land office business" selling her books and souvenir hatchet pins. But on the streets, she met little but ridicule, although she spat her share of invective in return. At the California Saloon at 10–12 East Broadway, the bartender threatened her with arrest; she referred to herself as a "defenseless gray-haired old woman. Your mother was a woman; would you call an officer to arrest her?" The bartender was reduced to pleading, "For God's sake, get out of here." Nation responded, "I won't. It's for God's sake that I came here," and she left on her own schedule after delivering a temperance lecture.

The California was among Butte's longest-lived saloons. The building was erected in 1877 and named the California in 1881, and it included its own brewery on the premises. When the original structure was torn down on June 10, 1905, the *Anaconda Standard* lamented, "With the tearing down of the California, to make way for a more modern building, Butte loses about the last of its real old historic landmarks…The old California had to go; the growing

demands of a prosperous community demanded it. The building which takes its place will be of stone—real stone—and brick." It had served as a general meeting place, town hall, house of worship, dance hall and theater; weddings and political conventions were conducted there before it became a beer hall in 1881, and it remained a central focus of the town thereafter. Vice President Thomas A. Hendricks, the first high federal elected official to visit Butte, was entertained there during his short tenure—he was vice president for only eight and a half months in 1885 before he died.

City hall with old California Saloon and Brewery at right, circa 1901. From *Souvenir History of the Butte Fire Department*, by Peter Sanger. *Scan by Butte–Silver Bow Public Library.*

City hall and second California Bar, circa 1965. The lot in the foreground is the site of the Butte Hotel that burned on August 9, 1954. *Photograph courtesy of the World Museum of Mining.* © *World Museum of Mining.*

A new California arose, and it was to this new saloon that Carrie Nation brought her hatchet and sharp tongue in 1910. That building survived until the entire corner block burned on June 24, 1969, when the saloon there was named the Board of Trade, the second location (and second fire) for that establishment. A parking lot marks the site today.

The ABC Saloon building was gone by the 1950s and remains another parking lot, but the angled sidewalk on the northeast corner recalls the front door where Carrie Nation made her entrance back in 1910. The Windsor brothel continued to offer its services to a declining population until 1968, when it was destroyed by a suspicious fire; the last madam insisted that it was set by the police when she failed to pay her monthly fee. The Grace ME Church still stands, abandoned, at Second and Arizona. Mountain View Methodist is still in use, and the Shortridge Church site is yet another parking lot in 2012.

Just two blocks north of the ABC Saloon, and seventeen years after Carrie Nation, a different development led to a game popular across the nation.

View of the 100 block of East Park about 1962, showing Crown Bar. All the buildings in that block are gone. *Photo by Clinton Peck, from Clinton Peck Collection, Butte–Silver Bow Public Archives, used by permission.*

Keno was invented at the Crown Bar, 110 East Park Street. A Chinese lottery called Pok Kop Piu, or White Pigeon Ticket, was well established in China and American Chinatowns, including Butte's. Entrepreneurial Chinese approached Pete Naughton, proprietor of the Crown Cigar Store in 1927, and began a lottery operation there, but a tong war developed that resulted in Butte police shutting down all Chinese lottery establishments.

Naughton's stepsons, Joseph and Francis Lyden, took over the operation with police blessing. By 1935, gambling was legal in Nevada, and Francis Lyden took the game to Reno, changing the Chinese characters on the lottery sheets to simple numbers. In Las Vegas, Joseph Lyden devised innovations including having drawings every quarter hour or so rather than once a day. By the mid-1950s, modern keno was well established.

The Crown was a "cigar store" in 1927, using the typical euphemism for a drinking establishment during prohibition. It occupied the east half of the first floor of the three-story Silver Block, built in 1897. Like many other saloons in Butte, the Crown offered tokens in change as a marketing ploy to bring customers back, since the tokens were only good at the business issuing them. The Crown was known officially as the Crown Bar in 1916–17 and as the Crown Cigar Store during prohibition. It continued as a restaurant until 1961 and was torn down about 1965. Today, a small privately owned park at the corner of Wyoming and Park Streets marks the site where keno was devised in 1927. The park is called Edna LaCass Park, memorializing Blond Edna, a madam whose brothel operated at 14 South Wyoming, around the corner from the Crown Bar.

Breweries in Butte accommodated a huge demand, beginning in 1876 when the Centennial Brewery was established on Silver Bow Creek. By 1899, the Centennial was spending $120,000 per year on 5 million pounds of Montana barley and had a $12,000-per-month payroll for one hundred employees. Leopold Schmidt, Centennial's founder, had left Butte by then, moving in 1896 to Tumwater, Washington, where he began Capital Brewing, the name of which was changed to Olympia in 1902.

For a time, there was another Olympia, also connected to Butte's Centennial Brewing. Butte's Olympia began independently in 1899. It stood along Silver Bow Creek where Harrison Avenue crosses it, but within two years, it was controlled by Centennial officers, who eventually shut it down in 1911.

Beer meant wealth and power—perhaps not as much as that generated by the copper kings, but enough for Centennial secretary-treasurer (and later president) Henry Mueller to become Butte mayor in 1891–92 and for his son, another Centennial president, Arthur Mueller, to build the massive Mueller Apartments on Granite Street as an investment in 1917. While no historic breweries still stand in Butte, the Mueller apartment building remains as a monument to their success.

In the late 1900s and early 1910s, five major breweries served Butte: Silver Bow-Crystal, Tivoli, the Butte Brewery, Centennial and Olympia. Montana voted for statewide prohibition in 1916, and in the run-up to its enforcement in 1919, the Butte Brewery promoted its flagship Eureka beer as "liquid food for temperate people." The Butte Brewery on North Wyoming

Crown Bar token from about 1917. *Author's collection.*

Butte Brewery on North Wyoming Street. From *A Brief History of Butte, Montana*, by Harry C. Freeman, 1900. *Library of Congress and Butte Public Library.*

Street, just a few doors south of the Finlander Hall, was the only Butte survivor of prohibition thanks to its Checo brand soda operation, and it remained in business until 1963. After a dearth of forty-four years, a new brewery opened in Butte. Hand-crafted brews are made by Quarry Brewing in the refurbished 1917 Grand Hotel, also known as the Wheeler Block for its ownership by the longtime U.S. senator from Butte, Burton K. Wheeler.

In another example of adaptive reuse, Headframe Spirits, a boutique distillery, opened in 2012 in the Schumacher Block, which was built in 1919 as a Buick dealership with a huge dance hall on the second floor, refurbished and still in use today.

CABBAGE PATCH TALES

The Cabbage Patch, a few blocks southeast of the central business district, was home to the dregs of society and those down on their luck. Alcoholics, bootleggers and criminals shared more than two hundred shanties with downtrodden minorities, widows with children and new immigrants who had just arrived to Butte with no connections. Three miners might share a cabin twelve feet square, alternating use of the bed according to the shift changes. There was no electricity, no running water, no sewer system save for the open sewer that ran through the heart of the neighborhood. Poverty combined with a wild diversity of ethnicities to make for a rough and tough area, avoided by most genteel citizens in prosperous Butte.

The Cabbage Patch became an easy target for squatters because ownership of its mine claims was unclear. Multiple landlords sometimes dunned residents for rent, with the result that tenants paid no one. Building neglect, as well as the practice of stripping vacant cabins for wood to burn or anything else of value, created a zone several blocks wide and long filled by dilapidated buildings—Butte's biggest eyesore.

Crime and disaster provide the only reliable reports about the Cabbage Patch. Mike Mahoney, who fancied himself the Beau Brummell of the Patch, had his one good shirt at Hong Huie's laundry on East Mercury Street, anticipating wearing it to the St. Patrick's Day celebration in 1909. Mahoney came off shift, got drunk and went to pick up his shirt. It wasn't ready. He flew into a rage, becoming "a one-man wrecking crew," and attacked laundryman Huie with a three-pound flatiron. It took the other laundry workers and some bystanders to save Huie, and Mahoney sat out that St. Patrick's Day in the city jail.

In the 1920s, "King of the Cabbage Patch" McNamara reportedly blew himself up with his own still, but bootlegging and making moonshine was by no means limited to the Patch. Home-based stills sprang up all over Butte during prohibition, and women were arrested nearly as often as men.

The Federal Housing Act, part of Franklin Roosevelt's New Deal, provided Butte with $1 million to demolish the Patch and erect low-income housing in Silver Bow Homes. At least 225 buildings came down in the spring of 1940, and Silver Bow Homes was opened on May 9, 1941. The Public Housing Authority manages more than two hundred two-story apartments there today; about $1.2 million in federal grants funded their 1979–80 renovation. Four pre-1890 shacks near the northern edge of the old Cabbage Patch survive and are operated today as small museums.

Little one-story rows of attached apartments similar to Silver Bow Homes, each measuring about twenty feet square, replaced the Florence Hotel on East Broadway with twenty units and the Mullins House in Centerville with twenty-two units in the late 1940s and early 1950s, but those two complexes are gone today.

RED-LIGHT DISTRICT

Butte's long-lived red-light district represents a loss to which many would say "good riddance." But like it or not, it was a vital element of Butte for more than a century.

No records exist describing the early ramshackle red-light area in Butte's gold rush days of the 1860s and the growing town of the early 1870s. As Butte became a populous, settled community, the services provided by ladies of the evening were in increasing demand, as was the case with every service.

By 1884, the district was centered on East Park Street, but growth meant more business blocks, and the district began to migrate one block south to Galena Street. In 1888, according to the euphemism for brothels on the Sanborn Fire Insurance maps of the day, eight "female boarding" establishments still operated on Park, but at least fifty-six single-story cribs

Venus Alley. The alternating door/window arrangement is typical of brothel architecture. *Photo by Arthur Rothstein, 1939, Library of Congress.*

could be found on Galena and adjacent Wyoming Streets. A concerted effort by city fathers in about 1890 to push the district many blocks to the southeast drove the heart of the district one more block south, to Mercury, but it did succeed in making them illegal in 1890—illegal yet tolerated so readily that brothels operated openly in Butte until 1982, thanks to payoffs to the police.

In 1916, brothels and cribs lined most of Galena Street from Main to Wyoming. Pleasant Alley, later called Venus Alley, lay between Galena and Mercury and was really the district's axis. Big parlor houses, including the Windsor, Victoria and Dumas, faced Mercury Street.

The Dumas Brothel, longest-lived of any surviving American house of prostitution, was erected in 1890 and offered its services until 1982. Declared "most endangered" by the Montana Preservation Alliance and by Butte Citizens for Preservation and Revitalization, this structure typifies brick construction during Butte's most sustained expansion—from 1882, when the gigantic Anaconda copper vein was discovered, until 1918, when the end of World War I caused a dramatic decline in copper demand.

In the middle of Butte's red-light district on East Mercury Street, the Dumas's leaking roof, collapsing brick and other damage made it a prime

Dumas Brothel Museum. *Photo by author.*

target for preservation and restoration. In 2007–8, Butte native John "Curt" Button donated nearly $30,000 to the local nonprofit preservation organization that oversaw roof replacement and critical interior masonry work to stabilize the Dumas. In 2012, it is threatened again, as a target for demolition to expand a parking lot.

Many other brothels have been lost. The infamous Copper Block, across Venus Alley from the Dumas, housed many ladies of the evening, and as recently as the 1970s, it was managed by "Dirty Mouth" Jean Sorenson, proprietor of the Stockman Bar in the corner of the Copper Block. On November 9, 1978, Sorenson shot twenty-year-old Gerald Lojeski in the Stockman. She served only three and a half years in prison, from 1979–82, and died at age seventy-eight in 1986.

The Copper Block went up in 1892, erected by the Nadeau family whose company owned five red-light properties. By the 1980s, it was vacant, and Seattle developer Allan Comp planned to spend $1.2 million to refurbish the building into an upscale restaurant and hotel. He received a $10,000 grant

Copper Block at Galena and Wyoming Streets. *Photo by Jet Lowe, Library of Congress.*

from the National Endowment for the Arts to bring nationally and locally known architects, artists and historians together in 1987 to brainstorm ways to make the refurbishment happen, but ultimately the project proved to be financially infeasible. By 1990, the Copper Block had reverted to the city/county for delinquent taxes.

The building was demolished in 1990–91 at a cost of $53,623; the intergrown nature of Butte's architecture resulted in partial demolition of an adjacent structure as well. A parking lot with a historic plaque and silhouettes commemorating the ladies marks the Copper Block site. Rick Griffith, a member of the Urban Revitalization Board that had sought to preserve the building, said, "Of all the buildings we've torn down, that one breaks my heart the most," according to the *Montana Standard* article of January 25, 1990, by John McNay and Eric Williams.

AT THE CHINESE MISSION

Butte's Chinese Baptist Mission was established in 1896 at 44 West Galena Street. Mrs. Whitmore was the superintendent there in 1898. By 1900, the mission had moved to a new structure at 24 West Mercury Street, across from the prosperous Wah Chong Tai Company. This block on the south side of Mercury in the heart of Chinatown developed quickly in the late 1890s and early 1900s. In 1891, a few log cabins, a corral and small stables, one house and a tin shop occupied the north half the block from China Alley to Colorado Street, facing Mercury. In 1916, sixteen buildings were there; today there are none. The last city directory listing for the mission is 1940, and the building at 24 West Mercury was vacant in 1942 and 1945; by 1948, all the buildings along that stretch were gone, and the entire block was a car dealer's lot in 1951.

Chinese children attended Butte public schools in the 1910s and '20s and received religious and other teaching at the mission. In 1918, it offered Sunday services from eight o'clock to ten o'clock in the morning and English classes every evening except Saturday and Sunday under the tutelage of Superintendent Earl Bracken; his regular job was as chief clerk for the Great Northern Railroad Freight Depot. The mission president was Mr. Ah Fong.

Dr. Wah J. Lamb, whose children appear in the photos here, was one of seven Chinese physicians practicing in Butte in 1918. He was among the first Chinese graduates from the University of Southern California Medical

Above: Inside the Chinese Baptist Mission at 24 West Mercury, 1919. Faith Lamb (front left) and Esther and Ruth Lamb (middle of center row) were Dr. Wah Lamb's children. The lady at left center is Mrs. Wong Cue, a tailor whose shop was at 103 South Main, and at right in the middle row is Mrs. Bracken, the superintendent's wife. The man seated second from left in the rear row is probably Hum Wing, a laundryman. *Mai Wah Society, donated by Dr. James Chung, used by permission.*

Left: Ruth and Johnny Lamb at their home at 1107 South Wyoming Street in 1918. Despite prejudice against the Chinese, there was a degree of assimilation, or at least toleration, for professional Chinese like Dr. Lamb and his family in Butte. Central Butte, where the Lambs lived, was largely northern European in its ethnic makeup. *Mai Wah Society, donated by Dr. James Chung, used by permission.*

School, in about 1896. Lamb's office then was at 116 East Mercury, and he and his family lived at 1107 South Wyoming, well outside Chinatown proper. Clearly, Dr. Lamb was doing well, as he advertised in Butte's newspapers nearly every day, as well as in the annual city directory. By 1928, Dr. Lamb was at 46 East Galena, and by 1940, he was retired and living in Los Angeles.

Other Chinese also resided well beyond the bounds of Chinatown. Hum Wing operated his laundry at 207 West Broadway, where he also lived. The building was a small house between the Baptist and Presbyterian churches on the corners of that block. The dwellings there were replaced by 1916 with the Montana Hotel, which burned down in 1988; the space is a parking lot in 2012.

Chinatown evolved and migrated from its core on Galena Street in the 1880s to early 1900s. Construction of the brick Wah Chong Tai building (1899) and adjoining Mai Wah (1909) anchored a relocation (encouraged by city fathers) to Mercury Street. Chinatown declined along with Butte, and with World War II, many Chinese left Butte for San Francisco and other coastal cities where they could find work in shipbuilding factories and other war-related jobs. By 1940, Butte's Chinese population was in double digits, perhaps 70 or 80, down from a peak in 1910–20 of 2,500, as estimated by Rose Hum Lee, a Butte native and expert on America's Chinatowns.

A MIDDLE-CLASS NEW YEAR'S EVE PARTY

The society corner in Victorian Butte newspapers recorded all and sundry events, including New Year's Eve parties. An item from the *Butte Bystander* for January 8, 1898, recounts such a gathering at the home of Mr. and Mrs. Erastus Thomas, 213 East Quartz. East Quartz is among the oldest parts of Butte, with Butte's first cabin supposedly built there in the 1860s. By 1900, there were fifty-eight dwellings in the single block bounded by Granite, Quartz, Arizona and Ohio Streets. Four were three-story boardinghouses, and six were two-story homes, four-plexes and apartments, while the rest were single-story homes; many of the latter had additional buildings that were likely inhabited. It is reasonable to estimate that the population in this block alone exceeded two hundred in 1900. Today, there are two surviving houses in this area.

The narrow single-story Thomas home was built between 1888 and 1891 as part of the Thornton Addition, so it was fairly new in 1897. The location was convenient, just two blocks north of Washington School, two blocks east of the Butte Brewery and immediately below the Parrot Mine complex, where Erastus worked as an engineer.

The 1897 New Year's Eve party list reveals the cosmopolitan nature of Butte. We can determine that the attendees came from all over Butte and from all walks of life. Mrs. Ellof Peterson managed a boardinghouse at 10 East Gagnon Street. Martin Brecke was a miner who lived at 725 North Montana. Michael Geiger, who attended with his wife and daughter, lived at 1109 West Woolman, where he ran the Home Industry Publishing Company. The "Bjorglums" on the list were probably Mr. and Mrs. Martin Bjorgum. He was a tailor with a shop at the northeast corner of Main and Mullins in Centerville, within the massive Mullins House–Union Hotel building complex; he and his family lived at no. 6 on O'Neill Street in Walkerville. Another tailor, George Erickson, worked for Henry Jonas at 11 East Granite Street but lived at 503 South Montana.

Mary Hoban, widow of John, boarded at 107½ West Quartz, The Sherman, which stood immediately west of the O'Rourke Building, in part of today's county jail parking lot. Another widow, Mrs. Albertine Minger,

Mullins House in Centerville. *Photograph courtesy of the World Museum of Mining. © World Museum of Mining.*

provides a connection to the East Side: she lived at the boardinghouse at the northeast corner of East Galena and Shields Avenue, just below the looming Pennsylvania Mine headframe at the southern margin of the Butte Hill. The two-story building there also was home to party attendees David Trotter (a machinist) and Louis Demars, both of whom lived there and operated a grocery store at the same location. Demars also ran a confectionery at 323 South Main (across from where Naranche Stadium is today). Today, the old corner of Galena and Shields is under the waste rock on the Berkeley Pit's rim just a bit northwest of the viewing stand; Shields Street has been significantly relocated.

The party list gives a cross-section of Butte's middle class, from tailors and grocers to engineers, publishers, machinists, miners, boardinghouse mistresses and widows living (apparently) independently. The *Butte Bystander* was a short-lived labor-oriented newspaper published from 1890 to 1898 as the *Butte Bystander* in 1890–97 and just the *Bystander* in 1897–98.

THE HIGH-CLASS WEST SIDE

The West Side neighborhood began with the Hub Addition in the 1890s and grew to become what passes for a "mansion district" in Butte. The area was not defined ethnically but rather by class, with middle-class clerks, mine foremen, businessmen, bankers, architects and other professionals forming the core community. But even the West Side has little miners' cottages, usually on the shady north-facing side of the street, across from stately Queen Anne mansions situated to catch the winter sun. Joseph Oppenheimer was one of the wealthier residents of the West Side, befitting his many business ventures. Even a frugal miner would not likely dabble in stocks and investments, but Oppenheimer used his wealth to leverage more, just as the copper kings did.

Joseph's parents, Elias and Mina Oppenheimer, emigrated from Germany and came to Butte from Salt Lake City in 1896. Their daughter married into the Symons family, prominent shopkeepers. Two Oppenheimers, including Joseph, and two Symons brothers founded the Symons Dry Goods Company, eventually occupying one of Butte's largest department stores. The first store, at 54 West Park, had fifteen employees and occupied eight thousand square feet, but success led to expansion by 1902 when the store boasted fifty thousand square feet. That store was consumed by a huge fire

Hennessey mansion at left and Kelley mansion at right, at the corner of West Park and Excelsior. Hennessey owned the Hennessey Department Store, the largest in Montana, and Kelley was a president of the Anaconda Company. These two homes survive. *Author's collection.*

on September 24, 1905, but the new Symons store in today's Phoenix Block rose from the ashes in 1906.

Oppenheimer was a major shareholder in the Butte-Argenta Copper Company, which he organized in 1906 in partnership with Henry Mueller, president of Centennial Brewing Company, and others to exploit old silver claims at Argenta in the Pioneer Mountains about fifty miles southwest of Butte. The Butte-Argenta Company had its Butte offices at #3 Lewisohn Building, which stood along Hamilton Street and faced Granite. The parking lot there today resulted from the fire in 1978 that destroyed the Lewisohn and Silver Bow Blocks.

Joseph Oppenheimer lived at 809 West Broadway, a large home in a prestigious block. In 1931, Oppenheimer's house was purchased and torn down by his neighbor, Andrew Jackson Davis, president of the First National Bank of Montana. Davis supposedly did it to expand his own home, seen by many as flaunting wealth during the Great Depression. Ironically, A.J. Davis countersigned the back of Oppenheimer's Butte-Argenta stock certificate. Among Oppenheimer's many interests, in addition to being treasurer of Symons Department Store and president of the Butte-Argenta Copper Company, was his own J.E. Oppenheimer and Company, dealers in fine cigars. His corporate secretary in that venture was Sylven Hughes, who in

Butte-Argenta Mining Company stock certificate issued to James Oppenheimer, one of the principals in the Symons Department Store and other business ventures. It is countersigned on the back by A.J. Davis, president of First National Bank. *Author's collection.*

1899 established the Olympia Brewery on Harrison Avenue where it crosses Silver Bow Creek. In 1914, Oppenheimer invested $25,000 in the Montana-Continental Development Company, a real estate firm. That was one-eighth of the business.

West Side mansions no longer support millionaires. Several, including the Hennessey on Park and the home of Anaconda Company president John Ryan on North Excelsior, have been converted into lodgings for Montana Tech students.

THE GIANT ELK

If anything symbolized Butte's over-the-top eclectic affluence, it might be the giant elk of 1916. Butte was near its peak population, 100,000, with more than 14,000 men working underground. The Fourth of July, a major holiday, coincided in 1916 with the statewide Elks assembly, which drew 30,000 members to Butte from across the state and beyond. Edmund

The elk erected for the Elks Convention of 1916, looking east on Broadway at Main, with the Hirbour Tower at left center. *Butte–Silver Bow Public Archives.*

Carns, a set designer for the Broadway Theater, created the $4,000 elk as an archway for the fraternal organization's parade. It was a wood-frame structure draped in wire mesh, cotton fabric and glue, painted and coated with copper-impregnated plaster. The elk's eyes were red ten-inch electric lights, and the Elks' traditional greeting, "Hello Bill," was illuminated on the creature's flanks.

The elk straddled the trolley line, and his antlers were sixty-two feet above the street, nearly two-thirds the height of the adjacent Hirbour Tower. It survived only a few weeks after the convention; funding to move it to the Columbia Gardens amusement park could not be found, and the elk's coat, containing $1,200 in copper, went to the smelter.

Part III

DECLINE

Certainly the ugliest town in the world.
                        —Time *magazine, 1928*

The most pictorial place in America.
                        —*Joseph Pennell,* Wonders of Work, *1916*

When World War I ended, copper demand and prices plummeted, and huge new reserves in Chile replaced Butte as the world's main copper supplier. This led immediately to economic depression and population decline in Butte, beginning in 1919 and continuing many decades. For the physical environment, slow abandonment and disrepair followed from the 1920s to the early 1960s.

THE ANACONDA ROAD

The year 1920 marks the precipitous decline, in fact the abrupt end, of the labor movement that had been at the forefront of Butte news since 1914. On April 21, 1920, striking miners were marching on the Anaconda Road, the primary artery that served the big mines on the hill. The Anaconda, Neversweat, St. Lawrence, Pennsylvania and Mountain View all employed between four hundred and six hundred men per shift in their heydays, and every day at shift change, thousands of men would pour down the Anaconda Road to its junction with Wyoming and Copper Streets to fan

Postcard view of the Butte Hill, with Corktown and the Anaconda Road in the foreground and winding up the hill. The Neversweat Mine is the one with seven stacks. *Author's collection.*

out to saloons, bars, boardinghouses, restaurants, churches and homes. The Anaconda Road also followed the lower reaches of Dublin Gulch on the eastern edge of Corktown and was lined by miner's cottages and boardinghouses full of Irishmen.

The 1920 strike, fomented by the radical Industrial Workers of the World, was apparently the last straw for the Anaconda Company. Armed gunmen came from the Neversweat Mine and began shooting into the mob of unarmed miners—at least that's the likely story, though the truth will never be known. Something like fifteen miners were shot as they ran down the hill, and two were killed. The event became known as the Anaconda Road Massacre, and it spelled the end of labor union activism in Butte for the next fifteen or more years.

The best known of the dead was Tom Manning, a twenty-five-year-old Irish immigrant who lived at the two-story boardinghouse at 20 West Quartz, the *Montana Standard* building's parking lot today. He intended to bring his wife and infant son to Butte from Ireland that fall, since he had nearly saved enough after three years of mining to do so. But he never got the chance; he lingered for nearly four days but died on April 25 as federal troops arrived in Butte to occupy the city and put down rebellious strikers. The troops stayed at the Florence Hotel on East Broadway while Tom Manning lay in state at

Decline

Soldiers pose on May 2, 1920, in front of the Florence Hotel, where they were billeted in the wake of the Anaconda Road Massacre eleven days earlier. *Butte–Silver Bow Public Archives.*

Tom Scanlon's house at 316 North Idaho, now a vacant lot. Scanlon was an IWW sympathizer, but sympathy for Manning went beyond the radical union; thousands came to the Scanlon house to pay their respects, and something like three thousand followed Manning's casket from St. Patrick's Roman Catholic Church to Holy Cross Cemetery.

In the wake of the Anaconda Road Massacre, union activism in Butte was quieted by the Anaconda Company's control, but union voices were not stilled. Ralph Chaplin, poet of the IWW, characterized it this way:

> *The overlords of Butte will not permit their right to exploit to be challenged. Drunk with unbridled power and the countless millions profiteered during the war, with lying phrases of "law and order" on their lips, the blood of workingmen dripping from their hands, and the gold of the government bursting their coffers, they face the nation unreprimanded and unashamed—reaction militant, capitalism at its worst. The copper trust can murder its slaves in broad daylight on any occasion and under any pretext. There is no law to call a halt. In the confines of this greed-ruled city, the gunman has replaced the Constitution. Butte is a law unto itself.*

BACK TO SCHOOL

The problem of what to do with school buildings in shrinking cities resonates with government officials, developers and preservationists today in places like Detroit and Philadelphia and other Rust Belt cities. It's been a problem in Butte since population decline began in 1919.

The end of World War I meant a crash in demand for copper, and while Butte's Anaconda Company was developing copper mines in Chile, what was good for the company might not be good for Butte. In the early 1920s, all Butte mines were closed for months on end and only restarted sporadically. The economic downturn meant that the new Finlen Hotel, intended to be a twin-tower building modeled after New York's Hotel Astor, would never be finished; the three-story stub on the east side of the hotel is the physical evidence marking the start of Butte's eighty-year decline, while the completed nine-story tower on the west, with its ornate Second Empire top and elegant Art Deco interior, mirrors the incredible opulence and thriving era that had just passed when it opened on January 1, 1924.

At least twenty-eight massive schools served 6,307 students in Butte and Walkerville in 1900, most of them in the uptown district; in the 1910s, population growth on the Flats to the south drove construction of three new schools in that area. Only four historic schools survive: Greeley, McKinley, Hawthorne and Sherman, and none is used as a school today.

Butte in the 1900s and 1910s was much like the rest of the United States in terms of grade school education, but the curriculum was rather different from that of the second half of the twentieth century.

Ninth graders took classes in Latin, rhetoric, American literature, algebra, bookkeeping and physical geography; by tenth grade, entire courses on Caesar were accompanied by German or French, civil government, algebra, zoology, English, English history and botany.

Juniors and seniors spent at least a semester studying Virgil, advanced German or French, Roman history, physics, world history, astronomy, geology, geometry, chemistry, American history and advanced English, and they had a choice between English literature and Greek.

Teachers were provided with a fifteen-page *Manual of Physical Culture*, giving instruction on exercises, from how to sit and stand to running, skipping, breathing exercises, wand drills, dumbbell work and more. "Marching will be given to all grades."

Decline

The schools were grand edifices, especially the public high school and the parochial school affiliated with St. Patrick's Roman Catholic Church. Butte's first high school stood between East Granite and East Broadway near Arizona. In 1885, Butte had fifteen schools in the city (most of them small), with 16 teachers and 956 students. Most classes were held at the original school at Broadway and Arizona, but that was a temporary situation while "plans [were] being perfected to build a grand system of school buildings in different parts of the city." Another large school, Central, in the block surrounded by Broadway, Dakota (then called Academy), Park and Montana Streets, also served Butte in 1885. Its teachers initially taught first through fifth grade, while upper-level classes were conducted at the high school on East Broadway.

Central School came down in 1893, and in 1894, that block was devoted in part to the new Butte Free Public Library at the southwest corner of Broadway and Academy. Charles Larrabee gave $10,000 to start the library, and Butte's citizens contributed $12,000 more; the city erected the building at a cost of $100,000 to the design of Butte's most prominent architect, Henry Patterson. By 1896, the library had 20,000 volumes and was adding 2,000 more annually; in 1948, 100,000 volumes were on the shelves.

The library sustained damage from embers blown from the devastating "million dollar fire" that destroyed the Symons stores a block east on Park Street on September 24, 1905, and it was severely damaged by fire on March 27, 1960, when the roof partially collapsed. Despite the destruction, architect Walter Hinick devised a reconstruction plan within the $155,000 insurance budget. The third floor, corner turret and front arches had to be removed, but the remaining structure was kept pretty much intact. The core of the old library remains under a modern façade in a building occupied by Western Montana Mental Health in 2012.

The library moved to its present location in the old telephone company building at Broadway and Idaho after 1988. When the Montana Theater was demolished, the telephone company built a new building on the site, and the public library moved into its old location next door.

The "new" high school built in 1897 replaced both the demolished Central Public School at Broadway and Academy and the other large school at Broadway and Arizona, which was renamed Washington School. The high school at Park and Idaho was replaced in the late 1930s by the current high school on South Wyoming, and the old structure burned down on April 10, 1946. A new parochial school was built on the site, to become part of the Butte Central Catholic School system.

Postcard view of Butte Public High School at Park and Idaho. *Author's collection.*

The original public high school between Broadway and Granite became Washington Junior High in 1898. Subsidence related to mining—Butte contained more than ten thousand miles of underground tunnels, and Washington School was right at the edge of the Hill—led to its demolition in 1913. The replacement school, on the same site, had a massive concrete foundation to alleviate the subsidence problems, poured using a huge tower and a one-hundred-foot chute in July 1914. It was so massive that it was a challenge to remove the slab when the 1913 school was demolished in 1977, so much so that the slab still underlies the site. In 2012, Washington School's location is a parking lot that annually becomes the craft area for the Montana Folk Festival.

St. Patrick's Catholic School stood just a block west of the public high school, at Park and Washington. It was built in 1888–89 and served for sixty-five years. In 1955, declining enrollments in the Catholic schools led to a major renovation of the building. The top floor was removed, and the exterior façade was modernized; virtually all of the Victorian ornamentation disappeared. It continued to be used by St. Patrick's as a junior high until about 2007. After a few years being vacant, what remains of the school building there was adapted into a high-tech research center for a Montana Tech professor working to commercialize a process that captures mercury from coal-fired power plants.

Postcard view of St. Patrick's Parochial School at Park and Washington. The lower two floors of the building survived though are much changed in their appearance. *Author's collection.*

Washington School between Broadway and Granite, east of Arizona, 1905. From *Annual Report of the Board of Education and City Superintendent of Schools*, vol. 18. *Scan by Butte–Silver Bow Public Library.*

Fires took their toll on Butte's schools. In addition to the high school in 1946, the Whittier school was completely destroyed by fire on February 2, 1953, and Meaderville's Franklin school, already closed by damage suffered in the 1959 Hebgen Lake earthquake, burned down on January 24, 1961. But over the decades, it was declining enrollments more than anything that reduced the need for a dozen massive schools all over Butte.

THE SHABBISHACKS CAMPAIGN

In May 1928, the *Butte Miner* headlined "City Cleanup Stirs Demand for Removal of Eyesores—97 Buildings Condemned as Fire Hazards." This was the start of the Shabbishacks campaign, probably Butte's first concerted effort to remove urban blight.

More than half of the condemned structures were occupied, but that didn't slow down the Better Butte Association of businessmen. For forty-five days, it ran photos in the paper of condemned buildings, together with owners' names and the tagline, "What Price Civic Glory?" By mid-June, 120 addresses were on the list; the campaign was promoted by a "Beautify Butte" float in the Fourth of July parade.

The most valuable ground occupied by a decrepit building was the Windsor on East Broadway next to the Hirbour Tower and, as the *Miner* pointed

SHABBISHACKS NO. 27

111-115 NORTH WASHINGTON STREET.
"Butte, Mont. F. E. McMakin and Rev. A. R. Coopman, Anaconda, Mont. Property located at 111-115 N. Washington St. Old dilapidated brick building, to tear down and remove within 30 days."—From description of CONDEMNED Buildings, City Engineer's Office.
WHAT PRICE CIVIC GLORY?
—TIDY TESS.

One of forty-five paid advertisements shaming owners of run-down buildings. *Butte Miner*, June 1928, located in Butte–Silver Bow Public Archives.

out to city fathers, almost across the street from city hall. The Windsor, however, was one of the few to survive Shabbishacks. It was destroyed in the Butte Hotel fire of 1954. The largest doomed property stood at Front and Arizona, a two-story duplex with stores on the first floor and lodgings on the second. The list included the Olympia Brewery buildings on Harrison Avenue, unused since 1911, as well as many houses throughout town.

By the time Better Butte's "educational and pictorial publicity" campaign ended on July 14, most of the condemned places were gone, willingly torn down by their owners within days of the legal notice. Historic preservation was nonexistent in 1928, and if there was any nostalgia for any targeted locations, it is not evident in the newspapers of the day. Those who fought condemnation proceedings likely only saw the potential loss of rental income. While it is certainly true that all these properties would have been considered historic today, there is also no doubt that in 1928, few people saw their loss as anything other than the march of progress—and that was a good thing.

There is also little doubt that most of the buildings were decrepit, dangerous, unhealthy and even falling down. Silver Bow County's population decreased

Before the fires, an aerial view of uptown Butte about 1928. *Photograph courtesy of the World Museum of Mining. © World Museum of Mining.*

from more than ninety-three thousand in 1918 to fifty-seven thousand in 1930, leaving many vacant homes, and early 1920s mine closures meant hard times for many who remained. People could not spend money to keep their homes repaired, a situation that has played out time and time again in Butte's boom-and-bust mining economy.

The Shabbishacks program spanned the town, from Walkerville and Centerville to Washoe Street across Silver Bow Creek. Homes were demolished at 315 North Idaho, 952 West Park, 515–517 West Broadway, 1038 West Mercury, 833 North Montana, 111–115 North Washington, 107 and 108 West Copper and at many other locations, most of which are still vacant lots today. As the campaign ended, W.A. Kemper, president of the Better Butte Association, wrote, "In our determination to help Beautify Butte, we shall continue to hew to the line, let the chips fall where they may!" Much of the debris from Shabbishacks demolitions was deposited at the southeast corner of Platinum and Excelsior Streets to build up the land there.

For the next twenty years, Butte and America had other things to think about than urban renewal; businesses and individuals alike fought the Great Depression and World War II. But the 1928 Shabbishacks effort would certainly not be the last in Butte.

MINES IN YOUR BACKYARD

The 1929 stock market crash came as Butte was recovering from its own depression, which began with the end of World War I when wartime copper demand fell and took Butte's economy with it. It took a few years for manufacturing to decline with the Great Depression, but the price of copper fell from eighteen cents per pound in 1929 to five cents in 1933, and that had a dramatic effect in Butte.

Toward the end of the decade, as Franklin Roosevelt's New Deal programs were beginning to show effects and the world's industry was gearing for another war, Butte became one of the locations documented by photographers hired by the U.S. government. Farm Security Administration (FSA) and Office of War Information (OWI) photographers fanned out across the country, first to document the impact of federal loans on farms and suburban developments planned by the Resettlement Administration. The project expanded to record lives of sharecroppers and migrant workers

Decline

and, eventually, general rural and urban conditions throughout the country. Butte was visited by several photographers working for this program in 1939–42.

What the FSA/OWI photos reveal about Butte is congestion and close juxtaposition of essentially unregulated industry and residential neighborhoods. The Butte Anaconda and Pacific electrified railroad hauled ore from the mines of Butte to the smelters at Anaconda, twenty-five miles to the west. In places, train cars passed almost literally within arm's reach of homes on the hill, and mine waste encroached on backyards. While this is an aspect of "lost Butte," it is one that few residents miss—although many people who were young then recall playing on the dumps and warming themselves on the compressed air pipes that fed the mine yards.

The mines themselves are part of lost Butte. A 1912 U.S. Geological Survey map locates 234 mine openings, all with names from Wake-Up-Jim to East Czarina. The Montana Bureau of Mines and Geology mapped 512 underground mine locations, 74 of them more than one thousand feet deep; 27 of those reached depths greater than three

Keeping laundry clean was a challenge with a mine in the backyard. *Photo by Arthur Rothstein, 1939, Library of Congress.*

thousand feet. All told, underground mine workings at Butte exceeded ten thousand miles in length, and most of those workings lay beneath about four square miles of surface.

Fifteen mine headframes dot the Butte area today. All the others were swallowed by the Berkeley Pit or have been bulkheaded and their surface locations landscaped, but many uptown Butte parks and neighborhood open spaces reflect locations of mines (Emma Park, Emma Mine; Cherokee Park, Silver King Mine). A house on Crystal Street is set into the waste rock from the Silver King, which shut down in 1910, but pyrite- and mica-bearing rocks still slough from the walls of that home's basement. The intertwined relationship of mines with residential areas is as much a hallmark of Butte as a mansion beside a boardinghouse.

View of the mines on the Butte Hill, circa 1905. The seven stacks of the Neversweat Mine are seen in the middle distance. St. Mary's church steeple is visible at right, at 713 North Wyoming. It was replaced in 1933 by a new church on North Main Street. *From a stereopticon view, courtesy Bob McMurray, Old Butte Historical Adventures.*

Decline

Mines operated day and night. People who lived on Alabama Street just below the Anselmo mine yard can recall lying in bed at night, feeling the vibrations of underground trams hauling ore to the shaft. Mining lies at the heart of Butte; Butte would not exist but for mining, and the now silent headframes—gallows or gallus frames to locals—speak loudly to that industrial heritage. When the Anaconda Company announced plans to remove them all to sell for scrap, retired miner and ropeman John T. Shea famously said, "You take down the first one, you'll hang from the second one."

Population decline affected all aspects of Butte life. In addition to schools, huge hotels suffered from low occupancy. The Arizona Hotel at Park and Arizona was built in 1917 and advertised all the modern conveniences: hot and cold running water in every room, steam heat and electric lights. It survived until 1964–65, when it was demolished, and a vacant lot marks its location. The Stephens Block, at the corner of Park and Montana, housed visitors until 1955, but unlike the Arizona, the Stevens survived. It was built by Deer Lodge businessman Frank Stevens in 1891. The second floor is

Arizona Hotel, circa 1918. *Butte–Silver Bow Public Archives.*

a relatively intact example of early twentieth-century hotel space: some rooms had sinks, likely added in the 1910s or 1920s, but all rooms shared a common toilet and bathroom. The original 1890s knob-and-tube electrical wiring served the Stephens in 1955 and is still visible today.

Willie Lindell lived in room 7 at the Stephens in 1891, and she worked as a waitress at the Theater Comique, a dance hall on Main Street just south of Park where part of the Metals Bank building stands today. "Waitress" was, to some extent, a euphemism for the multiple services available, but whatever she did, Willie made enough money to have her clothes cleaned professionally and attend performances at McGuire's Grand Opera House, but whether she saw Mark Twain when he performed there in 1895 is unknown.

One of the most dramatic fires of the 1950s destroyed the 1890s Butte Hotel on East Broadway on August 9, 1954. At the time, it was considered the worst fire in Butte's history, with a financial loss exceeding $1 million. The *Montana Standard* of August 10 reported that forty of forty-two "newly remodeled and ultra modern apartments" were occupied and that the fire left 125 residents homeless. The entire four-story front façade collapsed abruptly into Broadway Street during the blaze, but remarkably, no one was

Postcard view of Broadway, looking east, circa 1905. The Butte Hotel, destroyed by fire in 1954, is at center left. *Author's collection.*

Decline

Rialto Theater at Park and Main; it was demolished in 1965. *Butte–Silver Bow Public Archives.*

injured. In addition to the Butte Hotel Apartments, the Windsor Block, built as a hotel about 1886 and a survivor of the 1928 Shabbishacks campaign, was destroyed. The Hirbour Tower at the corner of Broadway and Main was threatened, and the heat started a small fire in the Hennessey Building elevator shaft, quickly controlled. A parking garage now occupies the site of the Butte Hotel.

A *Montana Standard* photo of the Rialto Theater being demolished was captioned, "The year 1965 was known not only as a year of progress, but one of demolition in Butte." The Rialto, at the corner of Park and Main, was erected in 1916 and hosted the first talking movie presentation in Montana in the 1920s. It replaced a conglomeration of mostly one-story buildings that included three saloons, three restaurants and four small stores. It was torn down to make way for the bank that occupies that corner today.

Part IV

ERA OF DESTRUCTION

An explosion of unknown cause and the fiery holocaust that followed it laid ruin to a sizeable portion of Butte's uptown business district early Monday.
—William J. Clark, Montana Standard, *February 29, 1972*

THE SIXTH FLOOR

One of the most prestigious and important buildings in Butte history, the Hennessey, is clad in deep red brick, adding to its imposing nature at the corner of Main and Granite Streets. Erected in 1897–98 where the Centennial Hotel once stood, the Hennessey was occupied in 1901 by the Anaconda Copper Mining Company and served as its corporate headquarters for the next seventy-six years. "The Sixth Floor" became a pejorative term for corporate greed and control.

A reporter in the 1920s characterized it this way: "Like the Lord God Almighty in His universe, the Anaconda Copper Mining Company is everywhere. It is all, and in all. Its titular Mercy Seat is on the sixth floor of the Hennessey Building at the intersection of Main and Granite streets, but it is enthroned in the heart, brain, and wallet of every man and woman from Nine-Mile to Stringtown, from the Main Range to Whiskey Gulch."

In reality, the Anaconda's control went far beyond Butte's bricks and mortar and mines, the only business powerful enough to be known simply as "the Company." Anaconda Copper eventually came to have great influence in—if not outright control of—Montana's legislature and courts, as well as

Hennessey Building at Granite and Main. *Photo by Jet Lowe, Library of Congress.*

over Montana's Congressional representatives and most of its newspapers. Montana in the 1920s was called a "corporate colony" of Anaconda Copper. An IWW songwriter known only as "Scottie" vilified Anaconda's president, Cornelius Kelly:

> *Of all the men in old Butte City*
> *That needs contempt or even pity*
> *There's one that rules on the Sixth Floor*
> *That's got them all skinned, by the score.*
> *This old gent's name is Cornelius Kelly,*
> *Was meant to crawl upon his belly,*
> *But listen, boys, he's good and true*
> *The Company's interests to pull through,*
> *But when it comes to working men,*
> *He'd rather see them in the pen,*
> *Or burning in eternal hell—*
> *His nostrils would enjoy the smell.*

The Company's fortunes and Butte's prosperity were intimately tied together. Even though the end of World War I led to a copper price crash and closing mines in Butte in the early 1920s, Anaconda was expanding. Chuquicamata and other mines in Chile and in Mexico yielded cheap copper for the Company beginning in the 1920s and remained vital operations until the 1970s. When the Anaconda Company was nationalized by Chile and Mexico in 1971, the company lost about two-thirds of its copper production and untold reserves. At the same time, the environmental movement in the United States was beginning to make freewheeling mining practices in Butte unacceptable. Strikes in the 1950s and 1960s, some lasting six months or more, also took their toll. By the late 1960s, Butte's economy was in a severe downturn.

Through the Company's ups and downs, its headquarters building stood firm. Minneapolis architect Frederick Kees designed the structure that housed the Anaconda Company, as well as Montana's largest department store, Hennessey's, on the first two levels and basement. The Hennessey Building was built to last. Even though it only stands six stories high, its internal frame is that of a skyscraper, supported by steel girders. Other buildings were not so fortunate.

MODEL CITIES

The Model Cities program was intended to be a showpiece of Lyndon Johnson's Great Society. Elements of the program made for long-lasting improvements in some target cities, but in others it created little and destroyed much. In Butte, it was in part an attempt to remedy the economic downturn, but results were mixed.

More than $22 million in federal funding allowed Butte to establish its Local Development Corporation and the Port of Butte, to build some housing and other projects and to promote the consolidation of the city of Butte and county of Silver Bow. One goal was "to improve the physical appearance of the Model Cities Neighborhood area by demolishing and removing dilapidated and deteriorated structures." That removal was accomplished, but whether it led to better neighborhoods is arguable.

More than $300,000 was allocated for demolition in the agreement signed on July 18, 1969, by Mayor Mario Micone. There is no evidence that cultural resource preservation figured in the plan, nor is there evidence of organized opposition to the idea of demolishing buildings by the hundred, most of them homes. Just as during the Shabbishacks effort in 1928, eyesores were eyesores, and removing them was progress.

Some three hundred buildings were demolished in the heart of uptown Butte in 1969–71, but virtually all the sites remain vacant lots in 2012. Two areas were targeted: a forty-nine-block zone mostly bounded by Arizona, Iron, Jackson and Mercury Streets and a twelve-block area north of Quartz Street between Main and Montana.

While small houses, often variants on the miner's cottage theme, were most represented in Model Cities demolitions, larger buildings fell as well. By the end of 1969, at least eleven brick and four frame four-plexes were gone, along with six brick six-plexes. The three-story Neely Apartment building at 301 North Main was among those the fire department considered to be the worst hazards; as it was demolished, falling debris damaged the adjacent National Market to the extent that it had to be removed even though it was not slated for demolition. Other accidents led to additional unplanned demolitions. The crews were busy: in one month, two crews accomplished seventy demolitions.

From boardinghouses to corner groceries, the old Butte lifestyle supporting 100,000 people had disappeared, and the architectural heritage underpinning

The Dorothy Block apartments at Granite and Wyoming. The house across Wyoming from the Dorothy was millionaire John Noyes's home. *Photograph courtesy of the World Museum of Mining © World Museum of Mining*

it was at a minimum unnecessary and in many cases unsupportable in the economic reality of 1970, when less than 42,000 people lived in Silver Bow County. The popular Dorothy Block at Granite and Wyoming contained fifty rooms, with three vacant in 1949, but twenty-three rooms were vacant in 1962. The Dorothy survived Model Cities but was torn down in 1978–79.

Long-lasting institutions such as the Knights of Pythias and other fraternal organizations declined with Butte's population and changing social dynamics. One of the last Model Cities demolitions removed the Pythian Castle at 127–129 South Main Street. City fathers were photographed in September 1970 examining the relics found in the building's cornerstone, but if anyone felt any remorse or nostalgia about the loss of the Pythian Castle, it was not recorded. In 2012, the vacant lot there boasts huge I-beams bracing the two adjacent buildings that the Castle once helped support. The

Sketch of the Pythian Castle at 127–129 South Main, built in 1900 and demolished in 1970. *Photograph courtesy of the World Museum of Mining. © World Museum of Mining.*

1900 cornerstone survives and sits in a yard at the corner of Broadway and Idaho Streets.

The four-story Pythian Castle had opened to considerable fanfare, touted as the most gorgeously furnished lodge rooms in the West, possibly excepting the Elks lodge in Seattle. It cost more than $75,000. The main lodge room was marked by golden oak trim and furniture—the latter with green silk upholstery—and an eight-foot-high seat for the lodge leader. Fabrikona canvas covered the paneled ceiling, and the walls were maroon. The exterior Romanesque style boasted "embattled parapets" of brick and wrought stone, and it occupied a typical footprint, 36 feet wide by 115 feet deep. Other organizations including the B'nai B'rith and the Butte Clerk's Union met in the Pythian Castle. It had survived a November 1955 fire, but ongoing deterioration got it listed among the buildings demolished under Model Cities.

Even the red-light district was pushed toward its end by Model Cities. Both the Victoria and Windsor parlor houses on East Mercury Street were torn down in early 1970. The Windsor, where May Malloy ejected Carrie Nation in 1910, had burned twice in 1968. The last madam and owner, Beverly Snodgrass, insisted that the fires were the result of her failure to pay her protection money to the police, but whatever the cause, the buildings were both gone by early 1970, listed on the Model Cities demolition rolls.

A compilation by Christopher Daly in 1992 found that 3,218 buildings were demolished in Butte from 1916 to 1954 and another 3,804 were torn down from 1954 to 1977.

NEIGHBORHOOD GROCERIES

Grocery stores dotted the uptown until the collapse of the economy, from the 1960s to 1980s, and long before the growth of big box stores. The city directory lists 201 grocers in 1918, 101 in 1960, 35 in 1979 and 5 in 2003. Most early groceries were tiny affairs, scattered throughout residential neighborhoods and the central business district. Arguably the most successful early store was Lutey's, which grew to have ten outlets in Butte, but its primary claim to fame is as the first self-service grocery in the United States.

The trademarked Lutey's Marketeria opened on February 7, 1912, in the first floor of the Stephens Block at Park and Montana. The self-serve approach was radical enough that Lutey's maintained a traditional store next door. Lutey's wholesale warehouse at 41–55 West Galena Street (in the former Montana Steam Laundry building) marketed to other grocers, as well as supplied Lutey's own stores; it also ran its own bakery and blended and roasted coffee there. A forty-eight-pound bag of sugar cost $4.05 in 1912, and ninety-eight pounds of flour ran $3.95.

Lutey's stores were established initially in Granite (now a ghost town) in 1889. In the wake of the 1893 silver crisis that decimated Granite, Joseph Lutey moved the operation to Philipsburg in 1895. Philipsburg depended mightily on silver mining as well, so Lutey finally relocated into Butte in 1897, where he and his sons built it into one of the largest grocery chains in Montana.

Joseph Lutey was a Cornishman born on Christmas Day 1849 in Morvah, a village about eight miles from Land's End at the far southwest tip of Great Britain. He came from a family of yeoman farmers and tinners, inasmuch as this part of Cornwall boasts both agricultural country and tin mines. Joseph's own background was in mining; he came to the

Sign on the south face of Stephens Block at Park and Montana, where Lutey's first self-service Marketeria was located. *Photo by Jet Lowe, Library of Congress.*

United States in 1868 (at age nineteen) and worked the mines of New York, New Jersey, Colorado and Nevada before landing in Montana at Granite in 1887.

The first Butte store was at 47 West Park (the Thomas Block that burned down in 1912). Joseph died in 1911, and the business continued under his sons until about 1924. At their peak, eleven Lutey's stores served Butte, with 350 employees. But there were no Lutey's in 1925. Irish fundraisers seeking money to help with Ireland's civil war (1922–23) approached Butte businesses for donations of $150 each. William Lutey refused; the ensuing boycott by Butte's Irish put them out of business, and Butte boasted no Lutey's stores after 1924.

The 2007 Chinatown Archaeological Dig (financial support from the Butte Urban Revitalization Agency; the exhibit is at the Mai Wah Museum, supported by the Montana Historical Society and Mai Wah volunteers) uncovered a large broken crock advertising Lutey's "fine pickles and pure vinegar" from the circa 1920 Chinese trash midden at the dig site, in the vacant lot south of Mercury and east of Colorado Street. Lutey's self-service

Both of these buildings on Granite Street across from the courthouse are gone. The building housing the Courthouse Grocery dated to about 1887, and the one to the left was built in about 1885. *Photo by Jet Lowe, 1979, Library of Congress.*

grocery was the model for Piggly Wiggly stores, the first widespread self-service chain in the United States.

While the Lutey's chain was prominent, little mom and pop groceries were probably more characteristic of Butte's neighborhoods. Two long-standing West Granite Street groceries both began about 1915. Courthouse Grocery, directly across from the courthouse, was established by D.W. McIntyre. The building his store occupied started as an 1880s residence. It survived into the late 1970s, when a new brick Courthouse Grocery replaced it on the corner, with a grand opening on February 22, 1980. Today that new brick building houses an office supply store. By 1980, it was clear that these tiny shops were vanishing: *Montana Standard* headlines in 1978 ("Neighborhood Stores Hang On") and 1982 ("Neighborhood Groceries Hang On") chronicled their early history but recognized a disappearing breed. The grocery at 601 West Granite, at the corner of Crystal Street, began in 1915 as Leonard Cook's Grocery and went through many iterations until it burned down as the Crystal Grocery on January 2, 1974. Despite temperatures below minus twenty degrees Fahrenheit, it took firefighters fourteen hours to completely control the fire in a small one-story brick building conjoined to a home to the west.

THE FIRES OF THE 1960S AND 1970S

It is difficult to point to one event that marked the start of the "era of destruction"—rampant fires of questionable origin. As we have seen, fire was a continual threat to Butte even with its fire-resistant brick. But the Anaconda Company's financial woes made the 1970s watershed years in terms of major losses, and among the earliest and largest was the J.C. Penney's Department Store fire on February 28, 1972.

The fire department was called at 12:21 a.m. on that cold morning to the corner of Park and Dakota in the heart of uptown Butte. By the time it was over, the intersection looked like "a wartime bombing scene." Besides the four-story Penney's building dating to 1916, twelve other businesses were destroyed, including the six-story Clark Hotel across Dakota Street. Arson was suspected but never proved. Total losses were estimated at a minimum of $3 million to as much as $5 million.

Butte resident Thomas Satterthwait wrote of the Penney's fire in the March 2, 1972 *Montana Standard*: "[I]t rends the heart to see a city, once considered a crown princess in western America, wither and die like a decrepit woman of the streets. The explosions and fire that tore at the heart of uptown Butte also tore at the hearts of her citizens." Feelings like his pervaded the town as loss after loss characterized the early 1970s.

Seventeen months later, on July 28, 1973, the huge Owsley Block (Medical Arts Center) at Park and Main burned to the ground along with two adjoining buildings with an estimated financial cost of $2.5 million. Both the Penney's and Medical Arts sites are parking lots today.

The Cooney Brokerage fire on March 18, 1974, caused an estimated $200,000 loss. The Pennsylvania Building at 32–44 West Park burned on August 20, 1975, a $290,000 blaze. And the 1978 fire that consumed the Silver Bow, Inter Mountain and Lewisohn Blocks was estimated at $2 million in damage.

The south side of the first block of West Granite Street seems fated to be vacant. In 1888, it was one of the last blocks in the central business district that did not yet contain new, large retail stores and office buildings. A small log doctor's office, a home and a small dressmaking shop, each measuring about twenty by thirty feet, occupied the Granite Street side, with a stable, a tiny sleeping room and four more small buildings scattered along the alleys and Hamilton Street (then called Utah). By September 1889, undertaker John M. Bowes was erecting a four-story office building on the site when fire erupted in the basement, ultimately consuming the block under construction, as well as Hennessey's Store on the southwest corner of Granite and Main. Across Granite, the Barnard Block's offices with lodgings above, together with the rear alley sides of Main Street stores south of Hennessey's, were severely damaged in a fire whose total loss was estimated at $512,000 in dollars of the day.

Three buildings were erected to fill this block in the aftermath of the 1889 fire. The Silver Bow Block began as two stories (1890–91) designed by architect J.C. Paulsen, but the spectacular upper floors were added in 1896–97 under the direction of prominent Butte architect Henry M. Patterson. The façade was granite on the lower floors and brick above, with decorative stone trim and paired windows in arches with Corinthian capitals forming mullions. Arches on the ground floor led to offices there and to the upper floors, reached by an open oak staircase that surrounded the elevator.

Patterson also designed the narrow four-story Inter Mountain Building in the middle of the block. Built in 1892, it was only twenty feet wide but nearly one hundred feet long. It was erected to house the *Daily Inter Mountain* newspaper, owned initially by Lee Mantle and then by the Anaconda Company from 1901 to 1913. For the next ten years, the paper printed there was the *Butte Daily Post*.

Henry Patterson came to Butte from Ohio about 1880, when he was twenty-four years old. His twenty-five-year career in Butte left its mark on more than two dozen surviving buildings, from homes and churches to hotels and business blocks. Many residents feel that the Inter Mountain was among the most beautiful of his creations. He left in 1905 for Los Angeles, where he specialized in churches and theaters.

The northwest corner of the block contained the Lewisohn Block, built to four stories in 1892–93, with a fifth floor added in 1908. Although the Silver Bow Block was two doors to the east, it was here in the Lewisohn Block that the Silver Bow Club had its rooms, on the fourth floor initially and on the fifth floor once it was completed. Mark Twain entertained club members here in 1895 and may have spent the night in the club's sleeping rooms. The Silver Bow Club, for Butte's richest men, built its own building at Granite and Alaska in 1906.

Silver Bow Block, Inter Mountain Building and Lewisohn (Professional) Building, circa 1965. All burned in 1978. *Photo by Clinton Peck, from Clinton Peck Collection, Butte–Silver Bow Public Archives, used by permission.*

On October 20, 1978, an early morning fire of undetermined origin apparently began in the Inter Mountain Building but spread quickly to the Silver Bow Block, whose multistory open stairwell apparently served as a fire chimney. Both buildings were destroyed. The Lewisohn Block (known as the Professional Building in 1978) only lost its upper floor in the fire, but structural damage meant that it would be demolished.

An earlier significant loss was the famous Beaver Block at the northeast corner of Granite and Main, where Wells Fargo Bank is located. Built in 1890, the three-story Marchesseau and Valiton Block was a typical Butte business structure, initially housing the Silver Bow National Bank, a grocery and a shoe store on the ground floor, with offices above. Henry Valiton was a native of Montbeliard, France, but came to America with his family in 1851 when he was nine years old. When he was eighteen, he headed west, working as a teamster, saloonkeeper and place miner in Colorado, South Dakota and Idaho before landing in Montana in 1866. He started his first livery business in 1867 in Deer Lodge and came to Butte in 1880 to maintain his own stable and invest in Owsley's much larger operation.

Henry Valiton's livery stable at the West Park Street Bridge (presumably the bridge over Missoula Gulch) rented barouches (fashionable carriages with collapsible hoods to protect the passengers from the elements), bench wagons, sulkies, covered carriages and saddle horses and claimed to have the finest hearse in Montana. The stable had a granite floor claimed to be superior to any other in Butte. Valiton served as Butte's mayor twice, in 1880 and 1890.

Marchesseau and Valiton's building was called the Beaver Block for the large copper and concrete beaver in its parapet. The last occupant, the Beaver Bar, closed its doors in the wake of the 1959–60 strike that idled mine workers for 181 days and was a serious blow to Butte's economy. Many mines, including the Anselmo, never reopened, and business after business shut down. Vacant for eight years, the building was slated for demolition, which began on October 7, 1968. The beaver had been removed and laid on the roof, to be given to the World Museum of Mining, but a fire broke out in the early morning of October 10. The beaver was destroyed in the roof's collapse, and the entire building lay in ruins within hours. No cause was determined, but the Beaver Block fire was labeled as suspicious.

In addition to the Board of Trade, other saloons also fell to fires, as well as to a smaller population that did not require 240 bars. The Atlantic was one of Butte's most famous drinking establishments, for its claim to "the longest

Upper façade of Beaver Block. *Photo by Arthur Rothstein, 1939, Library of Congress.*

The Beaver Block stood at Granite and Main until it burned during demolition in 1968. *Butte–Silver Bow Public Archives.*

bar in the world" if nothing else. Adolph Reichle came to Butte in the 1880s and, by 1889, was running a saloon at 62 East Park Street. His success was such that by 1893 he ran the City Hotel and its bar at 457 South Arizona together with another saloon at 214 East Park.

In 1895, Reichle began a long-term partnership with Arthur Schimpf in a saloon on the all-important northwest corner of Park and Main on the ground floor of the three-story Lizzie Block. Schimpf and Reichle's Saloon operated there for only a couple years until they built their own new building in 1897 at 56 West Park. That saloon was named the Atlantic in 1901 or 1902. The German heritage of the proprietors was reflected in their wares: in 1911, the Atlantic boasted that it was the only house in Butte to carry imported Muenchner Hofbrau and Pilsner Buergerbrau, together with family wines and—for medicinal purposes—a selection of the "oldest and finest brandies and whiskies in the world."

In Butte's heyday, the late 1910s, the Atlantic reportedly had a dozen bartenders "jumping like turkeys on a hot griddle" on a typical Saturday night. The bar was nearly the length of the narrow 110- by 20-foot building, reaching the alley between Park and Galena Streets. The Atlantic Bar continued at 56 West Park until 1926–27. During prohibition, which began in 1919 in Montana, a year before the national law went into effect, it was called the Atlantic Buffet or Café and offered "soft drinks," but it almost certainly sold illegal booze as well—most of the prominent Butte saloons did.

A new Atlantic began in 1940 a few doors to the east, at 46 West Park. That saloon was out of business after a February 18, 1969 fire destroyed the building. The building that housed the original Atlantic Bar from 1902 to 1927 (56 West Park) became various other shops and was housing Diana's Woman's Clothing when it was destroyed by an arson fire on October 14, 1974 (the first Diana's Shop fire).

THE COLUMBIA GARDENS

If fires like those at Penney's, the Medical Arts Building and many others in the business district tore at the heart of the community, the destruction of the Columbia Gardens was the kick to the gut that demoralized Butte's people more than anything. No tale of "lost Butte" can be complete without the Columbia Gardens, memorialized in several books and videos.

Copper king William A. Clark built the Gardens, opened in 1899 as a playground and respite from the smoke and dirt and toil of Butte that stood cheek and jowl with the mines. Whether Clark was purely altruistic in his motive is arguable; it is challenging to imagine that there was no hint of an attempt to buy goodwill as he fought and bribed his way into the U.S. Senate seat he coveted and finally won in 1901, but nonetheless the Gardens were built. A huge dance pavilion, a lake for boating, botanical gardens and arbors and, eventually, state-of-the-art rides and a roller coaster served not just Butte but visitors from hundreds of miles away.

After William Clark died in 1925, his holdings in Butte, including the Columbia Gardens, were sold to the Anaconda Copper Mining Company. The Company continued to operate the park at an affordable loss until the early 1970s. With the Anaconda's nationalization in Chile (1971), the Company was busy actively expanding the Berkeley Pit. By 1973, Company officials said that the Gardens stood in the way of mining that was vital to Butte's economy. The Gardens were closed after Labor Day 1973, and barely two months later, on November 12, a suspicious fire erupted that ultimately consumed most of the structures at the park.

Distrust of the Company had been building for years, and with the blaze a firestorm of protest, dissent and deepening distrust erupted. Many residents

Postcard view of Columbia Gardens pavilion and floral harp. *Author's collection.*

Boating on the lake at Columbia Gardens, circa 1905. *From a stereopticon view, courtesy Bob McMurray, Old Butte Historical Adventures.*

believed, and believe today, that the Columbia Gardens fire was set by the Company to preclude any possibility of rejuvenating the park. It also largely precluded and dispensed with the slight hope for a renaissance of Butte's heritage—to some extent, though, it also galvanized the public against the Anaconda's industrial machine. As Stacie Barry wrote in "Coming to the Surface," "The most enduring fire in the community consciousness is the destruction of the Columbia Gardens." The destruction of the Gardens was more than the loss of a recreational site; it was the loss of Butte's most central focus of pride, noted Barry.

By 1976, fourteen unsolved arson cases were on the books. Frustration led to squabbles between the state fire marshal and local authorities but not to any arrests in the major cases. Suggestions of arson led to lawsuits against *Time* magazine, which reported in 1975 that arson "has become common as people who are unable to sell their devalued buildings burn them for the insurance." But in fact, the motives—whether insurance fraud, some kind of grudge or actions of vagrants or thrill-seekers—remain unknown. What is known is that now Butte has a good collection of parking lots where spectacular historic buildings once stood.

Twenty major fires from 1898 to 1912 resulted in losses of $1.7 million in dollars of the day. The fires of the 1970s topped that figure almost every time a new major blaze hit: Penney's ($3 million), Medical Arts (1973, $2.5 million) and Silver Bow Block (1978, $2 million).

Not all fires were arson, nor even suspicious in the final analysis. Conditions in Butte's uptown deteriorated not just because of the economic downturn related to the Anaconda Company's troubles but also, ironically, to revitalized mining activity in Butte. The transition from labor-intensive underground mining to open-pit mining was completed during the 1970s. The need for lodging rooms for hundreds of underground miners no longer existed, so

Main Street in Meaderville, with Leonard Mine headframe looming behind. The Rocky Mountain Café was internationally known. Its magnificent bar has been preserved by the World Museum of Mining and is on loan to and in use by Headframe Spirits. *Photo by Arthur Rothstein, 1939, Library of Congress.*

upper floors of business blocks—formerly residential spaces—became vacant or were used as storage for the businesses on the ground floor.

Random storage in an old building with vintage (1915) electrical wiring set up the potential for disaster, but few business owners cared. Everyone expected the Anaconda Company to expand the Berkeley Pit to central Butte, and few if any building owners were willing to invest in improvements. They did not expect to receive a fair price for their existing property when hundreds of buildings fell to the Pit's growth.

Such concern was not unwarranted. By 1975, the Berkeley Pit had been expanding for twenty years, pretty much wherever the Company wanted it to. Whole neighborhoods and towns—Meaderville, McQueen and East Butte—fell to the wrecking ball or were simply buried in mine waste. Destruction of community spirit in ethnic neighborhoods was a factor in Butte's growing cynicism, even though for some it was a mixed blessing. Tales of corporate greed—taking with inadequate compensation family

All that remains of McQueen are the trees and streets in the middle distance of this view of Berkeley Pit in 1979. *Library of Congress.*

homes and institutions that had stood for nearly a century—contrast with stories recounting how glad some residents of Meaderville's ethnic Italian neighborhoods were to be relocated from ramshackle homes tens of feet from mines and mills to clean, tight homes and neighborhoods on the Flats or in McGlone Heights.

Fagan's Pharmacy

Fagan's Pharmacy at 52 Main Street in Meaderville was managed in 1928 by William F. Fagan, who opened the store in 1922 following ten years as a pharmacist in Butte. He dealt in "drugs, prescriptions, paints, and calcimine," the latter a white or tinted liquid containing zinc oxide, water,

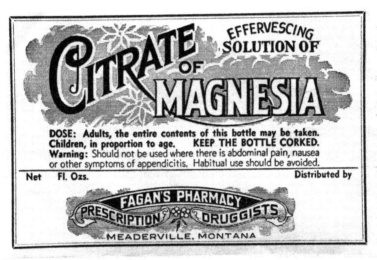

Labels from Fagan's Pharmacy. *Author's collection.*

glue and coloring matter and used as a wash or light paint for walls and ceilings. William appeared in Butte in 1913 when he was a druggist for Paxson and Rockefeller at 24 West Park Street. With his wife, Mathilda, he lived at various locations around Butte—412 South Dakota, 658 Travonia and 1109 West Galena—before moving to 77 North Main in Meaderville by the 1950s. He operated the pharmacy at least until 1954; the establishment continued as Farrens Village Drug and Sundries until the location was vacated in 1961. The Fagan family relocated to 2209½ Cottonwood in 1963 as Meaderville was destroyed by expanding Berkeley Pit operations.

Fagan's was at the corner of Main and Noble Streets, a few hundred yards from the Leonard Mine. The Combination Mine—not operating by 1916 but soon rejuvenated as the Reins Shaft of the Leonard—was even closer, up the street to the north adjacent to the Italian mission at 76 Main. Two saloons flanked Fagan's to the north, another stood to the east on Noble Street and yet another was across Noble to the south.

The large two-story building across Main from Fagan's housed a saloon (53 Main Street), a moving picture theater (55 Main) and a restaurant (57–59 Main), with a meeting hall above them in 1916. By the late 1920s, Teddy Traparish, Peter Antonioli and Louis Bugni had established the first Rocky Mountain Café at 53 Main. That building burned down in 1940, and the Rocky Mountain Café moved down the street where it enjoyed huge success and international renown. The Rocky Mountain Café was closed in 1961 as the Pit grew, but the back bar survived—Traparish gave it to the World Museum of Mining. In 2011, the museum loaned it to Headframe Spirits distillery (21 South Montana), where it is in use once again.

A TALE OF TWELVE CHURCHES

Despite Butte's rowdy "wide open town" reputation, churches have always had an important role in the community. Two churches once guarded the northern corners of the intersection of Copper and Alaska Streets, but today these are vacant lots.

The northwest corner (101 West Copper) held the Scandinavian Methodist Episcopal Church, built between 1891 and 1900. The church was actually on the second floor, with housekeeping rooms on the first level. The building survived until 1982, but the upper floor was vacated before 1951, when the building was being used as a two-flat apartment on the first floor only.

This 1939 view of the northern part of the business district includes the area around Quartz and Alaska Streets. The forty-five-foot church spire at left is the Scandinavian Church that stood at Copper and Alaska, and the mine in the background is the Original. *Photo by Arthur Rothstein, 1939, Library of Congress.*

The opposite corner, 51 West Copper, was home to Gold Hill United Lutheran Church (later Gold Hill Norwegian United Church). In 1890, this corner was occupied by a one-and-a-half-story house, probably a small four-square building like the others in this block. The two-story church building was erected there by 1891 but was vacant then; the church occupied the structure by 1900, and a dwelling—presumably the minister's—was in the basement. This church was gone by 1951. The new Gold Hill Lutheran Church is at 934 Placer Street today.

Two mines gave their name to the Gold Hill Church. Gold Hill No. 1 had a shaft on East Copper, opposite the southern end of Pennsylvania Street. It was worked in the late 1890s and reactivated in the 1930s. Gold Hill No. 2 was between Copper and Quartz Streets, just east of Montana, where the new (2003) county jail stands. It began in the late 1880s but was idle in 1900 and probably never operated again.

Ethnic pride and sense of community often centered on the local churches, and this spirit also led to some early preservation efforts—not "historic preservation" per se, but simply a matter of saving an important community feature. The best example is St. Helena's Church, erected in 1921 to serve Meaderville's Italian Catholic community. The World Museum of Mining began in 1963 and opened its doors in 1965, intending to preserve memories and educate the public about mining and the culture associated with it in Butte. It quickly became a repository for much more than artifacts: entire buildings were moved to the thirty-three-acre museum grounds, where they form the centerpieces of a model mining community. St. Helena's Church is the largest such moved structure. The Mining Museum also preserves a model home ("Superintendent's House") and other original buildings from Butte's past—out of context, but saved.

Butte's Serbian community began to conduct religious services in 1897, and its first Holy Trinity Orthodox Church was erected at Porphyry and Idaho in 1904–5, the second Serbian Orthodox Church built in North America. Archbishop Tikhon of Moscow, head of the Orthodox Church in America, traveled to Butte from New York City to dedicate Holy Trinity on December 16, 1906. By 1910, the church was serving a Serbian population of more than four thousand, and eventually Serbians counted as many as ten thousand or more in Butte. Subsidence in shallow tunnels from the nearby Emma Mine and damage sustained during the 1959 Hebgen Lake earthquake resulted in demolition of the 1904 church. A new one went up in 1964 on Continental Drive, including the traditional onion dome style that was present on the original church.

Shortridge Christian Church, where Carrie Nation held forth in 1910, dated to April 1893. The land cost $3,065 in 1891—an "inflated" price, according to financially strapped church elders—and the structure itself cost $10,000, plus $2,000 more for the furnishings, all for an initial congregation numbering about two hundred. The stained-glass windows were donated. Sarah E. Shortridge, longtime executive secretary of the national Christian Women's Board of Missions in Indianapolis, supported the church philosophically if not financially, and it was named in her honor. After more than half a century, in the face of financial problems at the church and Butte's declining population, the Drama Guild of Butte bought the building and used it from 1959 to 1968. A fire of unknown origin destroyed the church in May 1968. Ellen Crain, then in fourth grade at the nearby parochial school, remembers vividly the fire's multicolored smoke: red, green, yellow and blue, possibly from burning sets and paints from the Drama Guild. The space is a parking lot today.

African Americans had two churches in Butte. One African Methodist Episcopal (AME) church stood on the northeast corner of Mercury and

Postcard view of Shortridge Christian Church, Washington at Mercury. *Author's collection.*

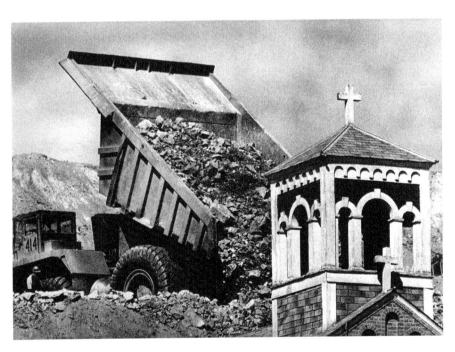

Burying Holy Savior Catholic Church in McQueen beneath waste rock from Berkeley Pit, 1977. *Photo by Walter Hinick,* Montana Standard, *used by permission.*

Idaho, but it became the Baptist Bethel Church before 1916 and later was a Pentecostal mission; it was demolished in about 1959. The second AME church, Shaffer Chapel at Platinum and Idaho, was built in 1901 and is among the few surviving small churches, in use as a day-care center in recent years.

The Congregational Church on Granite Street, across from the courthouse, both built by 1884, survived for a while as the Carpenters' Union Hall, but by 1906, when the Carpenters' Union built its massive new building, the church was gone. The German Church on Silver Street between Colorado and Dakota became the Jewish Orthodox Synagogue in the early 1900s after the B'nai Israel Temple was built in 1903 and the reformed and orthodox Jewish communities separated. The building survived until the 1950s. Nearby, the Swedish Mission Church at Dakota and Porphyry succumbed to the expanding Emma Mine and was gone by 1951; today, this entire block is Emma Park.

Outside the "Church Zone" on the West Side, both Sacred Heart on East Park and Holy Savior in McQueen fell to Berkeley Pit expansion. Walter Hinick's iconic photo showing waste rock burying Holy Savior Church captures the conflict between industry and economy and the central emotional needs of the community. Some former McQueen residents cannot see this image without tears in their eyes thirty-five years later.

LOST NEIGHBORHOODS

Butte's ethnic palette suffered from the ongoing population loss, as well as the homogenization that prevailed across America by the 1940s and 1950s. First-generation immigrants were becoming parents and grandparents. In Butte, the ethnic character of many neighborhoods lives on even though the physical locations may have been lost to the Pit.

Thirty or more ethnicities called Butte home. Meaderville was Italian. McQueen was Slovenian, Austrian and Croatian. Williamsburg was German. Chinatown was obviously Chinese. The East Side included Lebanese, Irish, Montenegrins, Serbians and more. But these neighborhoods were not sharply delineated; Italians lived in British Walkerville, and Finns lived in Irish Corktown.

The Anaconda Company's wartime newspaper, *Copper Commando*, records the following names as McQueen residents in a special edition from November 24, 1944: Ceserani, Jovick, Pirnat, Favero, Bertoglio, Mandich,

Halse, Laity, Mitchell, Massey, Brocco, Pagliano, Dobel, Patrick, Vicivich, Rozich, Pedrovich, Bailey, Treolar, Tomich, Stepan, McCauley, Quilici and Davis. McQueen was multiethnic though predominantly eastern European. Kathy Koskimaki Carlson recalled:

> *As a Finnish Lutheran growing up in an Irish Catholic neighborhood [St. Mary's], I remember young friends taking me into the church and explaining all the mysterious features—holy water fonts, confessionals, candles, catechism class—and visiting the convent on errands. It was a true family, that neighborhood, and when my mother was ill, we were recipients of many kind gestures. Whether the impetus was "good works" didn't matter; our family was enriched by our exposure to that culture, which we may have missed out on if we'd lived in traditional Finntown. We got to experience both.*

Meaderville, McQueen, East Butte and the Columbia Gardens neighborhood are the most noted neighborhoods completely destroyed by Pit expansion, but the East Side, Finntown, Dublin Gulch and others were severely affected and are represented by only a handful of buildings today.

Meaderville lost 488 buildings. A few were relocated to streets on the Flats, but most were demolished. McQueen counted 330, and East Butte lost 344. Hundreds more fell in the neighborhoods to the west, even though the Pit did not expand to swallow them up—the threat was enough to result in abandonment, neglect and demolition.

Meaderville's demise was precipitous, following hard on the 1962 fire that destroyed Meaderville Mercantile. By late 1964, essentially all of Meaderville was abandoned and its people relocated—some to the Flats, some to the West Side and some out of Butte.

RELOCATE THE TOWN

By the early 1970s, the Company's expansion plans indicated the need to remove the entire central business district. Study after study accepted that idea axiomatically. In 1972, the Butte Regional/Urban Design Assistance Team (RUDAT), composed of American Institute of Architects and local professionals, spent three days analyzing Butte, with the ultimate recommendation—perhaps not surprising from architects who would reap the benefits of an entire redesigned and relocated city—being to move uptown Butte to the Flats.

Their alternatives were anemic: rather than move the business district purposefully, let the slow movement to the Flats continue—the tacit assumption being that it would certainly happen one way or another. Their other alternative was "walking away from the whole thing, allowing it to become another (largest ever) Ghost Town." While acknowledging that it seemed unlikely for such an end, "it could happen if steps are not taken immediately to prepare the plan for 'orderly withdrawal' from the present city site to the new planned communities."

Butte Forward arrived in this climate of a dire need to get out of the Anaconda Company's way, together with the fear created by the huge fires of the early 1970s (J.C. Penney's moved off the hill "because of too many fires there"). This nonprofit organization was apparently bankrolled by the Anaconda Company and Montana Power Company and was formed to press the city into making the move happen. In May 1976, the city council had approved the relocation concept and the associated eventual demolition of everything in the central business district. All that remained was to select the site. While the rest of the nation celebrated the bicentennial, Butte wrestled with a huge question: where to move an entire city.

The Anaconda Company pledged $11 million to the relocation, estimated to cost $50 million total. On the same page in that July 3, 1976 *Montana Standard*, the merger of Anaconda with the oil company Atlantic Richfield (ARCO) was announced. Ironically, on a later page, Carmen Winslow reported on a visit to Butte by preservationist Alan Minscoff, who spoke to a small group at the Copper King Mansion about saving historic buildings. But saving old buildings was not on the list for Butte Forward and the Anaconda Company.

Weekly council meetings debated where to relocate, but there seemed to be no serious opposition to the basic fact that the move would happen until Beverly Hayes and other business owners established Save the Central Business District and began to agitate not for any particular relocation site but for the rejection of the whole idea. Florist Aggie Jean Golubin, a member of the business group, said, "Look around you. These old buildings are antiques and showplaces. Other cities fix up their old buildings. They plan on tearing ours down."

Hayes alleged the move to be a benefit only to the Anaconda Company, not to the business community or to Butte. "If we can't get the Anaconda

Company to respect us as individuals," she said, "where will they stop? They already got the Columbia Gardens; now they want to destroy Butte."

The community was suddenly, and somewhat surprisingly, polarized. For the first time, people were challenging the Anaconda Company's ultimate authority. In "a tumultuous meeting" on July 21, 1976, the city council voted to halt the relocation plan and to stop seeking federal funds to support it. Mayor Mario Micone and Butte Forward president Shag Miller went to Washington, D.C., the next day, but the project was dead in the water; the federal government was not interested in participating in something that significant numbers of local citizens opposed. So the heart of uptown Butte was saved.

It is difficult to assess the full impact on the populace of a corporate anaconda constricting the community, a century of sloppy and environmentally unfriendly mining practices, continual losses of community icons and a generally depressed economy. One blow after another continued from the 1970s into the 1980s. The Anaconda Company, struggling to make ends meet, sold itself to Atlantic Richfield in 1977 when petroleum companies could barely find enough things on which to spend their surging profits.

Environmental problems and Chile's control of the copper market meant that ARCO's new acquisition faced unanticipated expenses and severe competition, as well as low prices for its primary commodity, copper. Within five years of the purchase, ARCO had shut down the last remaining underground mines and the smelter in Anaconda, as well as the huge Berkeley Pit, eliminating more than three thousand jobs in a matter of months. Butte's economy took another nose dive. Even with the development of a smaller pit at the base of the East Ridge—a mine still in operation today—the town was at best able to maintain a status quo business climate. And the fires continued.

One of the last major uptown landmarks to be lost to flames was the five-story Montana Hotel that stood on West Broadway between the Baptist and Presbyterian churches. The sandstone lintel bearing the carved inscription "The Montana" was saved and now serves as a bench along the sidewalk bordering the parking lot between the churches. Butte was so inured to the idea of arson that by March 1988, when the Montana was destroyed, the phrase "arson is suspected" was being repeated in news articles until a final verdict of destruction by accident was handed down. Butte's Urban Revitalization Agency (URA) had the Montana Hotel on its agenda for discussing methods of attracting investors to rejuvenate the vacant building, but after the hotel burned, the URA approved a grant for $9,500 to help pay for its demolition—it was deemed to be damaged too much to restore. And Butte had another parking lot.

Although Butte held (and holds) remarkable upscale business blocks, huge hotels, beautiful theaters and a healthy number of mansions, Butte has always been a working-class town. Of the six thousand contributing historic properties in the Butte-Anaconda National Historic Landmark District, the vast majority are peoples' homes, from single-family houses to distinctive Y-porched walk-up duplexes on Galena Street. Because there are so many present, it is sometimes challenging to argue for keeping one more little house, but their losses have ultimately destroyed neighborhood fabrics and the integrity of streetscapes.

The losses of the 1970s and 1980s were not without value. In a 1981 report to a Washington, D.C., conservancy group concerned about the destruction of resources of significant historical importance, URA director Janet Cornish wrote that "the problems of arson and vandalism have surfaced as a unifying force," in part as the community began to recognize the value of historic structures to economic development. The city and private groups

Housing on North Montana Street, circa 1970. Three distinct buildings contained five apartments each, demolished in about 1975 to create a five-space parking lot. *Photograph courtesy of the World Museum of Mining.* © *World Museum of Mining.*

initiated a reward fund for help in the arson cases, fought to change zoning rules to discourage the storage situations that led to some fires, created an arson hotline and began a coordinated effort to secure and mothball vacant buildings to reduce the likelihood of fires, both accidental and intentional.

The Urban Revitalization Agency, funded through tax increment levies and charged with renovation and rehabilitation in and around the central business district, was established in 1979, the same year the city/county invited a federal Historic American Engineering Record (HAER) survey to contribute to a rehabilitation action plan. Combined with ARCO/ Anaconda's announcement in 1978 that any expansion would not "take out the uptown," a signal seemed to be sent that uptown Butte's historic buildings were worth saving and maybe, just maybe, even worth restoring and being returned to viable use. These attitudes contributed to a positive view of historic properties that led to development of the Regional Historic Preservation Plan in 1993 and to the creation of a grass-roots citizens' preservation organization in 1994.

Part V

THE BATTLE FOR BUTTE

Looking back I saw Butte on her fabled Gold Hill still lit like jewelry and
sparkling on the mountainside in the blue morning dawn.
—Jack Kerouac, 1949 (published in Esquire *magazine, 1970)*

B eginning especially in the early 1990s, awareness and at least a
slight reduction in the economic depression led to a rise of historic
preservationism, for its own sake and as a vehicle for economic development.
The fourteen-year struggle to expand the NHLD to largest in the nation
was accomplished through the efforts of many, spearheaded by Ellen Crain,
Chere Jiusto and others. An active grass-roots organization, Butte Citizens
for Preservation and Revitalization, helped save several significant structures
from the wrecking ball, including the Acoma and the O'Rourke.

In 1992, a programmatic agreement was signed by representatives
of the Butte–Silver Bow, Anaconda–Deer Lodge and Walkerville city
governments; the U.S. Environmental Protection Agency; the Montana
State Historic Preservation Office; the Advisory Council on Historic
Preservation; the Montana Department of Health and Environment; and
ARCO. The deal called for development and implementation of a Regional
Historic Preservation Plan (RHPP), and in 1993, a thick volume with data
and proposals came out, funded primarily by ARCO. The plan was an
attempt to outline the challenges and possibilities of preserving, managing
and promoting a huge historic district that coincided with a huge Superfund
site while also generating new economic development. The document
challenged the absolute supremacy of Superfund; while acknowledging

the needs of environmental safety and restoration, it required that Butte's architectural heritage be honored.

Nineteen years after the RHPP was issued, significant environmental restoration had been done, together with an expansion of the National Historic Landmark District to combine Butte, Anaconda and Walkerville into a single district containing more than six thousand contributing historic properties, making it the largest NHLD by that count. Interpretive trails were established. Millions of dollars in Urban Revitalization Agency money (at about $1 million per year in the late 2000s) had been leveraged to rehabilitate many commercial and residential properties, and major historic resources such as mine yards, the railroad and smelter facilities had been initially protected thanks in part to state, federal and other grants.

The volunteer nonprofit Butte Citizens for Preservation and Revitalization provided more than $30,000 in more than fifty awards to help with property improvements over a dozen years. Outside investment in major commercial buildings resulted in significant economic development through adaptive reuse, as in the Sears building, dating to about 1912, which one hundred years later included three floors of apartments, uptown's first grocery store in many years and a science museum in the basement. Residents overwhelmingly voted for a $7.2 million bond issue to rehabilitate the 1900 fire station that housed the Butte–Silver Bow Public Archives and to build an attached state-of-the-art archival vault.

Despite the positive developments, the historic district remained under threat in the 1990s and early 2000s. Butte's historic preservation office, the first in Montana, had no teeth, and buildings continued to be lost.

More than three hundred historic properties were lost to fires, neglect and demolition between 1961, when the Butte Historic District was established, and 2006, when it was expanded. At least 104 demolitions from 1989 to 1996 cost the city/county $550,463, and many of those demolition sites remain vacant lots or parking lots. While these demolitions were presumably done under the Community Decay Ordinance and represented neglected buildings that the city/county considered dangerous or damaged beyond repair, they were losses to the historic district nonetheless.

In part in response to these losses, Butte was put on probation as a Certified Local Government (CLG), and its historic status was listed as threatened. To return Butte to a CLG in good standing, one requirement from the state was the enacting of a comprehensive historic preservation ordinance, which was accomplished in March 2007 in the face of some significant opposition in the community and on the city council. The new ordinance allowed for a voluntary protective Local Register for historic properties and empowered the seven-member appointed Historic Preservation Commission to define and review designs for work on historic properties and to review all demolition requests. Demolition denials could be—and regularly were—overruled by the city council.

The Butte-Anaconda National Historic Landmark District contains some six thousand contributing historic properties, about four thousand in Butte and two thousand in Anaconda. All are automatically listed in the National Register of Historic Properties, and consequently, Butte–Silver Bow finds itself in the peculiar situation of having only fourteen independently listed National Register properties. In large measure, this is because Butte was designated a National Landmark so early (1961).

While Missoula County contains about seventy-one independently listed National Register properties and about twelve additional NR districts, Silver Bow County has fourteen independent and four thousand contributing—which technically are all equal, but the reality is that an independent listing goes through more rigor and review. Butte could have many hundreds of independently listed National Register properties, but they are already there because of the National Landmark District. The small number of independently listed properties has sometimes been used to argue for different management of Butte's historical resources—an idea that is based on faulty logic and a failure to appreciate the nature of the historic district. The public seems to have a hard time accepting that a wide range of buildings and structures with varying historic associations and in various forms of condition can all be considered worthy of preservation.

Even being one of the fourteen independently listed properties provided no protection to one of them. In 2007, despite the new Historic Preservation Ordinance, the 1917 Longfellow School was torn down. Longfellow was one of three schools dating to the 1910s that joined the National Register in 1988. It was designed by architect Wellington Smith in Collegiate Gothic style, including sandstone and terra-cotta trim on its brick façade. The crenelated parapet and Tudor arch entry typified the style, used mainly on public buildings such as schools and university construction. The school on the Flats was important both for its architectural style and for its role in Butte's first real suburban development as the population swelled to near 100,000 in 1917. The trolley system reached the neighborhood where the Longfellow stood in

Longfellow School in 2007 shortly before its demolition. *Photo by author.*

1916, allowing growth to take off. The school was built for $55,000 and opened for use in September 1917.

As enrollments declined, the Longfellow School was closed in 2001. An initial purchase offer fell through, and a local developer bought the property for $60,000 in June 2007. In November, the city/county allowed demolition to begin without prior demolition review by the Historic Preservation Commission, as required by the Historic Preservation Ordinance. After demolition began, meetings and threats of lawsuits followed, but ultimately the elected city/county Council of Commissioners allowed the demolition to proceed. Twelve new residential units now occupy the site.

The fight over the Longfellow School demolition pitted preservationists in the community and on the Historic Preservation Commission against the local government, and the relationship among these players remains strained and confrontational at times. And now Silver Bow County has thirteen independently listed National Register locations.

After the 2007 Historic Preservation Ordinance was enacted, the Historic Preservation Commission (HPC) approved more than forty demolitions with little or no fanfare and denied about five, mostly with great fanfare. Of those five, two are still standing.

In 2008, an owner applied for a demolition permit to tear down a contributing property on the lot adjacent to the home where he lived on West Silver Street. Meetings and discussions went nowhere; the owner was unwilling to consider any options, such as trying to sell it, because he didn't want neighbors. The case went to the Council of Commissioners, which, as was its right, overruled the HPC's denial and allowed the demolition to go forth. The council meeting where the decision was made included one commissioner berating preservation and preservationists, characterizing them as "out-of-state do-gooders." He said that the demolition approval by the HPC was "wrong, immoral, unethical and it just stinks." Two volunteer HPC members, one a lifelong Butte native, resigned from the HPC as a result, citing the reason allowed for the demolition, namely to give the owner a bigger yard. The debacle also helped catalyze the eventual resignation of the local historic preservation officer.

The next battle, in 2009, was somewhat more controversial, in part because the properties in question in the 300 block of South Idaho Street were listed as "neutral," as neither contributing nor noncontributing to the National Landmark District. "Neutral" is not a category in use today, but it was valid in the late 1970s and early 1980s when the most recent inventory of historic properties in Butte concluded. The HPC invoked a ninety-day hold on demolition to recategorize the properties, which included one of the few surviving alley houses in Butte, dating to about 1889. The main house, on Idaho Street, was constructed in about 1888 and became the home of John H. Foote, president of the Troy Laundry Company, in about 1904. The HPC, with concurrence of the Montana State Historic Preservation Office, determined that the properties were contributing elements to the Landmark District and denied demolition. Ultimately, on appeal to the Council of Commissioners, the demolition denial was overturned, and the building sites became landscaping adjacent to a new medical office building.

The two examples here were high profile, with at least nine articles, letters and editorials in the *Montana Standard* regarding the Silver Street house and nine more regarding those on Idaho Street. But they pale in comparison to the fight over the Greek Café.

The Greek Café

In 1917, Butte's population peak, East Park in the single block from Main to Wyoming boasted ten saloons, nine restaurants and stores of every stripe, from grocers to furniture dealers. Most contained lodgings above ground-floor retail establishments. East Park Street was the primary gateway to the core of Butte's central business district. The new two-story business block erected by heirs of Louis and Herman Gans and Henry Klein on the southwest corner of Park and Wyoming in 1917 replaced seven separate one-story shops and bars that dated to about 1890. Gans and Klein were Jewish clothiers from New York and Helena who never lived in Butte, with their main Butte store at 120–122 North Main Street.

The new building contained diverse storefronts within one edifice that held a large hall on the second floor. The second-floor hall probably eventually became a meeting and dining room for Butte's Greek population; it bears the label "Greek Café 2nd Floor" on an old map. Greeks never numbered much more than a thousand or so in Butte, but they established several restaurants and groceries and held Greek Orthodox services in the

Miner's Union Bar/Greek Café in 1965. *Photo by Clinton Peck, from Clinton Peck Collection, Butte–Silver Bow Public Archives, used by permission.*

old Welsh Presbyterian Church (at Aluminum and Dakota Streets) from 1960 to 1977.

Six storefront entrances, three on Park and three on Wyoming, gave access to restaurants, saloons, grocers and other shops. The Hazelwood Café at 84 East Park became the Tia Juana Chili Parlor in 1930 and operated for the next twenty-two years. In the 1950s and 1960s, it was the Tasty Lunch for about fifteen years before its final incarnation as the Corned Beef and Turkey Plaza Restaurant. Next door, 86 East Park, held a barbershop from 1918 to 1969, when it was vacated. Thomas Stamatis ran a fruit shop on the corner, 88 East Park, from the 1920s to the 1940s, and Sevores Grocery followed at that location until about 1960.

The Wyoming Street side initially had another café at 5 South Wyoming, evolving from the Butte Chili Parlor to Wyoming Café to Hamburger King in 1939, when it probably became part of the adjacent Miners Union Bar, accessed at 7 South Wyoming from 1937 to 1954. The Miner's Union met in the hall upstairs at times during the 1930s, 1940s and early 1950s. During prohibition, the saloon was a "soft drinks place" but almost certainly offered liquor as well, as did most pre-prohibition saloons in Butte. The last storefront on the street (11 Wyoming) was a secondhand store at least from 1928 into the 1940s. The building was erected with upper bearing walls three bricks (twelve inches) thick, a steel roof truss and cast-iron columns marking storefronts.

The entire Park Street corridor suffered from Berkeley Pit expansion in the 1960s, as the main route into uptown Butte shifted to the south and the interstate that was developing there. The Greek Café building was effectively abandoned about 1970. Decades of neglect took their toll. Most of the roof collapsed sometime before 2002, and the building was evaluated as dangerous. The county, which owned it thanks to unpaid taxes, offered it to developers, but all projects fell through. In 2008, the county issued a challenge to the preservation community: find a way to finance restoration or the building will be demolished.

In early 2009, Nicole von Gaza and Mitzi Rossillon, on behalf of Butte Citizens for Preservation and Revitalization, applied for and won a $30,000 Challenge Cost Share Program grant from the National Park Service to help stabilize the Greek Café building. The application was the highest rated of any in the Rocky Mountain Region. Butte–Silver Bow's Urban Revitalization Agency committed $95,000 as part of the project to roof the building, and in 2010, Butte CPR obtained nearly $45,000 in federal stimulus money allocated by Montana's state legislature to historic preservation projects for additional stabilization.

In January 2011, the city/county invited developers to propose redevelopment projects. The only respondent planned to invest about $700,000, essentially preserving the outer shell and building a new structure within it, if the city/county would stabilize the structure using the grant funding and URA commitment. The first and only bid to stabilize the Greek Café that the city/county received came in $100,000 over the funds available and $120,000 over the engineer's cost estimate, in part because delays placed the challenging stabilization project in the middle of the busy and short construction season. The bid was rejected and the project readvertised with bids solicited for either stabilization or demolition. When the Council of Commissioners added the possibility of demolition, that action contributed to the loss of the $45,000 stimulus grant money. To partially compensate for that loss, Butte CPR offered $20,000 that would go toward a stabilization project only.

Ghost sign lost when the Greek Café was demolished in 2011. *Photo by Jet Lowe, Library of Congress.*

One bid for stabilization was submitted, at $78,840, and one for demolition came in, at $93,438. After contentious discussion, the Council of Commissioners accepted the stabilization bid, but the URA Board then decided not to support the developer's loan request and matching grant. Without that support, the developer withdrew his proposal. Although the designed stabilization project would ensure that the building would continue to stand for at least three more years, during which time another developer might be sought, the council voted to demolish the building. This was despite the fact that demolition would cost nearly $15,000 more than stabilization.

During August and September 2011, more contentious discussions continued as those interested in the building's preservation hoped to garner wide public support to hold off demolition. A public rally supporting the preservation of the building took place, and a request for a judicial injunction to delay the demolition was denied. On Columbus Day, October 10, a preservation advocate chained himself to the Greek Café, but upon his removal, the demolition began. Within four weeks, the building was gone.

The Greek Café story was reported in at least ninety-two newspaper articles, editorials and letters to the editor, and it was on the agenda for the Council of Commissioners for at least twenty of its weekly meetings. The Montana Preservation Alliance, the National Park Service and the National Trust for Historic Preservation all wrote letters supporting the stabilization of the building, but to no avail. Today a vacant lot occupies the site.

THE THREAT IN 2012

It surprises visitors to Butte to learn that iconic buildings continue to be threatened. Another high-profile case involved the M&M Saloon, built in 1890 and open twenty-four/seven until 2003, when renovation required locks to be installed. The owner, in conflict with his financial backer, attempted to auction off the contents, from the original 1890s bar to the bar stools and historic safe. In the face of a huge outcry from Butte citizens, the financial backer prevented the auction from happening, and today a new owner has done significant revitalization and has the bar and restaurant open once again.

The *Anaconda Standard* called the new Carpenters' Union Hall "a model" when it was begun in 1906, reporting that its interior would be "arranged specially to afford convenient meeting places for organizations." It was to be constructed of "brick with granite trimmings," but when it was finished, its entry arches and windowsill courses included many slabs of Montana sandstone, quarried near Columbus and noted for its fine, uniform grains deposited in rivers about 78 million years ago.

A spat between the building owners and the regional carpenters' union threatened the hall with demolition in 2012, but it seems to be safe for now. Apart from its architectural interest, the Carpenters' Union Hall has seen its share of notable visitors.

Most students of Butte history know about one notorious woman's visit to Butte in 1910. Carrie Nation brought her hatchet but had little impact locally beyond entertainment. Another woman, prominent in her day, also visited Butte in 1910: Emma Goldman.

Not entirely a household name today, Emma Goldman was indeed well known nationally in 1910, as an anarchist, anti-religion zealot, advocate for birth control and homosexual rights and more. Butte culminated her five-month 1910 tour, which her manager boasted "had not a single encounter with the police." Among her previous run-ins with the police was an arrest

Carpenters Union Hall, West Granite Street. *Photo by Jet Lowe, Library of Congress.*

in 1901 following President William McKinley's assassination by anarchist Leon Czolgosz. Goldman admitted meeting Czolgosz but disavowed any connection with his act; she was released two weeks later after "third degree" interrogation.

In Butte at the Carpenters' Union Hall on Granite Street, Goldman spoke in June 1910 on "Francisco Ferrer and the Modern School." Ferrer was a fellow anarchist and educator, executed in Spain because the church feared his teachings, according to Goldman. Her second speech focused on "The White Slave Trade," by which she mostly referred to prostitution. Butte had quite a reputation in that area, of course, but it was a nationwide issue.

Goldman came to Butte three more times, in 1912, 1913 and 1914. Although she was an American citizen by virtue of marriage, her husband's citizenship was revoked, and courts held that this invalidated Emma's as well. She was deported to Russia (her 1869 birthplace was in Lithuania, at the time a part of the Russian empire) in 1920. She had become known as "the most dangerous woman in America." Disillusioned with the Soviet experiment, she left in 1921 and spent the rest of her life—not quietly—in Europe and Canada. She died in 1940.

Preservation in general in Butte is an ongoing battle with "progress," even when there is nothing in the offing to replace a demolished building. Possible changes in the Historic Preservation Ordinance would weaken it. Despite the well-documented economic value of intact historic neighborhoods, it's a real challenge to find the funds to save neglected buildings.

CULTURAL TOURISM: THE FUTURE?

It would be a serious mistake to read of all the losses described here and envision a Butte with nothing but bare bones, vacant lots and vacant, boarded-up houses. The National Landmark still contains six thousand contributing historic properties, about four thousand in Butte. Nearly intact streetscapes such as West Granite in the heart of Butte and Center Street in Centerville combine with individual gems of history, from the Copper King Mansion to remnants of the Cabbage Patch, to portray much of Butte's past, warts and all. Even streets with many empty holes, making for toothless stretches, still harbor houses that miners, clerks, widows, tailors, Irish families, Italians, Serbians, Cornishmen and so many others called home. Butte's architectural heritage has suffered and is threatened, but it persists.

The Mai Wah Society came about in the early 1990s with the groundswell of grass-roots energy dedicated to saving as much of the past as possible. The organization took ownership of two of three surviving Chinatown buildings and created a museum to promote and interpret Asian cultural heritage in the intermountain west. Its growth has seen an important Chinatown archaeological dig in 2007, sponsored by the Urban Revitalization Agency, that uncovered more than 60,000 artifacts, the most important of which are now on display. In 2010–12, the Mai Wah partnered with the Montana Heritage Commission in Virginia City to return to Butte 2,500 artifacts and cabinets dating to the 1890s. They had been moved to Virginia City in about 1945 but now are on loan in their original location at the Wah Chong Tai Mercantile.

In 2004, the historic Prohibition era speakeasy beneath the Rookwood Hotel on Main Street was rediscovered. Historians were aware of the speakeasy, but it had been neglected for decades. Entrepreneurs took advantage of increased appreciation for Butte's history and had the place

The Mai Wah and Wah Chong Tai buildings. *Photo by Jet Lowe, Library of Congress.*

open as a museum within weeks. In 2011, the tour company spawned by that rediscovery took more than three thousand visitors around Butte, emphasizing historical accuracy on guided tours of eight privately restored historic spaces.

Butte and southwest Montana were the venue for the 2009 national Vernacular Architecture Forum, attracting 225 architects, planners, historians, guides, folklorists and preservation specialists from thirty-four states, Canada and Malaysia. The three-day program showcased Butte in one of the first conferences the organization had held west of the Mississippi in its thirty years. One attendee, from North Carolina, summed up her visit to Butte by saying, "It changed my life." Reactions like that encourage historians, tour guides, preservationists and planners.

A new history-based tour company began in 2011, offering golf cart excursions. Combined with walking tours, the chamber of commerce trolley and self-guided walking or driving tours, visitors have multiple ways to experience Butte. Longtime historical attractions such as the World Museum of Mining, Our Lady of the Rockies, the Mineral Museum at Montana Tech and the Granite Mountain Memorial interact with tour companies to work toward a unified approach to heritage tourism in Butte.

Butte in 2012, two years short of its sesquicentennial, is not a ghost town nor is it a museum. It is not the thriving metropolis it once was nor has the vision of a comprehensive heritage park become anything like reality. Cultural tourism seems to be drawing increasing numbers of visitors and their money, but not in numbers sufficient to truly drive the economy, and the struggle to preserve what remains so that future tourists and future Butte residents can enjoy it remains a battle. The money needed to rehabilitate and reuse four thousand or more buildings simply is not there, and even with a relatively stable population, the demand is not there either. And even when money and demand are both there, the battle between those who would create parking lots and those who would save for the sake of history can become bitter and prolonged. Will Butte's international ethnic, labor and mining history remain at the level it is today fifty years from now?

Ultimately, what Butte has lost is what every American city has lost: life and times that no longer exist. Butte's surviving buildings echo those days more loudly than in many cities, and if Butte has lost a lot, it is because it had a lot to lose. What remains is far more than a shell or a relic. What remains is a living, breathing city with its heritage on its sleeve, still clearly in evidence, waiting to be retold...if it can survive.

SELECTED BIBLIOGRAPHY

Astle, John. *Only in Butte: Stories Off the Hill.* Butte, MT: Holt Publishing Group, 2004.

Barry, Stacie. "Coming to the Surface: The Environment, Health, and Culture in Butte, Montana, 1950–2010." PhD diss., University of Montana, 2012.

Baumler, Ellen. *Spirit Tailings.* Helena: Montana Historical Society Press, 2002.

Brinig, Myron. *Wide Open Town.* Helena, MT: Sweetgrass Books, 1993. First published 1931.

Butteopia.com. *Butteopia.* Silver Street Group Limited, 2006.

Byrnes, Mike. *The Mules, the Mines, and the Miners.* Butte, MT: Old Butte Publishing, 2004.

Calvert, Jerry W. *The Gibraltar: Socialism and Labor in Butte, Montana, 1895–1920.* Helena: Montana Historical Society Press, 1988.

Crain, Ellen, and Lee Whitney. *Images of America: Butte.* Charleston, SC: Arcadia Publishing, 2009.

Dean, Patty, ed. "Coming Home: Butte and Anaconda, Montana." *Drumlummon Views* 3, no. 1 (2009). Drumlummon Institute and Montana Preservation Alliance.

DeHaas, John N., Jr. *Historic Uptown Butte*. Bozeman, MT: privately published, 1977.

Doig, Ivan. *Work Song: A Novel*. New York: Riverhead Books, 2010.

Duaime, T.E., P.J. Kennelly and P.R. Thale. *Butte, Montana: Richest Hill on Earth, 100 Years of Underground Mining*. Montana Bureau of Mines and Geology map, Butte, Montana, 2004.

Emmons, David M. *The Butte Irish: Class and Ethnicity in an American Mining Town, 1875–1925*. Urbana: University of Illinois Press, 1989.

Everett, George. *The Butte Chinese*. Butte, MT: Mai Wah Society, circa 1998.

———. *Butte Trivia*. Helena, MT: Riverbend Publishing, 2007.

Finn, Janet L., and Ellen Crain. *Motherlode*. Livingston, MT: Clark City Press, 2005.

Freeman, Harry C. *A Brief History of Butte, Montana*. Chicago, IL: Henry O. Shepard Company, 1900.

Gibson, Richard I., ed. *Vernacular Architecture Forum Guidebook: Butte and Southwest Montana*. Butte, MT: Vernacular Architecture Forum, 2009.

Gibson, Richard I., and Irene Scheidecker. *Historic Stained Glass in Selected Houses of Worship, Butte, Montana*. Butte, MT: Butte Citizens for Preservation and Revitalization, 2006.

Glasscock, C.B. *The War of the Copper Kings*. Helena, MT: Riverbend Publishing, 2002. First published 1935.

Kearney, Pat. *Butte's Catholic Family*. Butte, MT: Skyhigh Communications, 2010.

————. *Butte's Pride: The Columbia Gardens.* Butte, MT: Skyhigh Communications, 1994.

————. *Butte Voices: Mining, Neighborhoods, People.* Butte, MT: Skyhigh Communications, 1998.

Lee, Rose Hum. *The Chinese in the United States of America.* Aberdeen: Hong Kong University Press, 1960.

Lutey, Kent. "Lutey Brothers Marketeria." *Montana: The Magazine of Western History* 28 (1978): 50–57. Montana Historical Society, Helena, Montana.

MacLane, Mary. *I, Mary MacLane: A Diary of Human Days.* New York: Frederick A. Stokes Company, 1917.

————. *The Story of Mary MacLane.* Chicago, IL: Herbert S. Stone and Company, 1902.

MacMillian, Donald. *Smoke Wars.* Helena: Montana Historical Society Press, 2000.

Malone, Michael P. *The Battle for Butte: Mining and Politics on the Northern Frontier, 1864–1906.* Seattle: University of Washington Press, 1981.

McGlashan, Zena Beth. *Buried in Butte.* Butte, MT: Wordz & Ink Publishing, 2010.

Montana: The Magazine of Western History, issue devoted to Butte, Montana (2006). Montana Historical Society, Helena, Montana.

Murphy, Mary. *Mining Cultures: Men, Women, and Leisure in Butte, 1914–41.* Urbana: University of Illinois Press, 1997.

O'Daly, Hugh. "Life History of Hugh O'Daly, Written by Himself at the Age of 78 Years." Unpublished typescript at Butte–Silver Bow Public Archives, circa 1945.

O'Malley, Richard K. *Mile High, Mile Deep*. Livingston, MT: Clark City Press, 2004.

Punke, Michael. *Fire and Brimstone: The North Butte Mining Disaster of 1917*. New York: Hyperion, 2006.

Rickey, Les. *The Bad Boys of Butte*. Butte, MT: Old Butte Publishing, 2004.

Shea, Debbie Bowman. *Irish Butte*. Charleston, SC: Arcadia Publishing, 2011.

Shovers, Brian. "Remaking the Wide-Open Town: Butte at the End of the Twentieth Century." *Montana: The Magazine of Western History* (1998). Montana Historical Society, Helena, Montana.

Shovers, Brian, ed. *The Speculator: A Journal of Butte and Southwest Montana History*. 2 vols., 4 nos. Butte, MT: Butte Historical Society, 1984–85.

Swibold, Dennis L. *Copper Chorus*. Helena: Montana Historical Society Press, 2006.

Vincent, Matt, and Chad Okrusch. *Butte Then and Now*. Charleston, SC: Arcadia Publishing, 2011.

Walter, Dave. *More Montana Campfire Tales*. Helena, MT: Farcountry Press, 2002.

Wheeler, Burton K. *Yankee from the West*. Garden City, NY: Doubleday & Company, 1962.

World Museum of Mining. *Mining in Butte*. Charleston, SC: Arcadia Publishing, 2011.

Writer's Project of Montana. *Copper Camp*. Helena, MT: Riverbend Publishing, 2002. First published 1943.

INDEX

ABOUT THE AUTHOR

Richard I. Gibson is a geologist, historian and tour guide in Butte, Montana. He leads historic walking tours for Old Butte Historical Adventures and drives the tourist trolley for the Butte Chamber of Commerce. He has served on the local Historic Preservation Commission and as education director at the World Museum of Mining, and he is currently the secretary of Butte Citizens for Preservation and Revitalization. He also serves on the Mai Wah Chinese Museum Board and wrote the guide to the Mai Wah Archaeological Dig Exhibit. Gibson edited the guidebook for the 2009 Vernacular Architecture Forum in Butte and wrote most of the Butte section and two essays. He contributed eighteen columns on historic architecture to the *Montana Standard* newspaper and is the author of the Butte History blog, http://buttehistory.blogspot.com.

Photo by Kathryn Langmyer Henderson.

Visit us at
www.historypress.net
....
This title is also available as an e-book